D1372718

Let's be true to ourselves even when it ain't pretty.

Let's fuck up and make messes, laugh and love. Let's become our own heroines.

In this unblushing guide to personal growth, author Lux Alani draws on her dominatrix experiences to offer cheeky, kink-think wisdom—covering topics like authenticity, confidence, body image, resilience, and courage—using life lessons and practices found in the taboo world of BDSM. With its simple but essential message of empowerment, *The Little Vanilla Book* is the perfect gift for a woman to give herself and her girlfriends for ongoing inspiration. So, embrace some stiletto swagger and uncover the surprising truth that kink wisdom isn't just for kinksters—with the right mindset every woman can use a little BDSM spirit to wake up her inner truth (latex catsuit optional).

THE
LITTLE *V*ANILLA BOOK

THE
LITTLE *VANILLA* BOOK

S&M Wisdom to Improve Your Everyday Life

Lux Alani

ATRIA BOOKS
New York London Toronto Sydney New Delhi

BEYOND WORDS
Hillsboro, Oregon

ATRIA BOOKS
An Imprint of Simon & Schuster, Inc.
1230 Avenue of the Americas
New York, NY 10020

BEYOND WORDS
20827 N.W. Cornell Road, Suite 500
Hillsboro, Oregon 97124-9808
503-531-8700 / 503-531-8773 fax
www.beyondword.com

Managing editor: Lindsay S. Easterbrooks-Brown
Editor: Anna Noak
Copyeditor: Sylvia Spratt
Proofreader: Jenefer Angell
Cover design: Devon Smith
Composition: William H. Brunson Typography Services

First Atria Books/Beyond Words hardcover edition October 2015

For more information about special discounts for bulk purchases, please contact Simon & Schuster Special Sales at 1-866-506-1949 or business@simonandschuster.com.

The Simon & Schuster Speakers Bureau can bring authors to your live event. For more information or to book an event, contact the Simon & Schuster Speakers Bureau at 1-866-248-3049 or visit our website at www.simonspeakers.com.

Manufactured in the United States of America

10 9 8 7 6 5 4 3 2 1

Library of Congress Cataloging-in-Publication Data

Alani, Lux.
   The little vanilla book : s&m wisdom to improve your everyday life / Lux Alani.
      pages   cm
   1. Self-actualization (Psychology).   2. Self-acceptance.   I. Title.
   BF637.S4A533   2015
   155.3'3391—dc23

                    2015003285

ISBN 978-1-58270-571-2
ISBN 978-1-5011-1058-0 (ebook)

For the quirky, lovely, burdened, pure *force*
who was my mother; who would have choked on her tea,
then tried out a life spank.

Contents

'Cause I'm a woman
Phenomenally.

—MAYA ANGELOU,
"Phenomenal Woman"

A NOTE FROM Lux

Hey lovely sisters! Get ready for potent and cheeky life lessons and heart-to-heart wisdom. My mission is to inspire you to claim your power and divinity. I want to help you past S&M taboos so that my message can reach you. I understand your concern about taboos, I'm vanilla, too. (I'm also an experienced crisis counselor so feel free to freak out, I've got you.)

The thing is, I practice radical openness to empowerment, because who wants disempowerment? I base my choices on whether they deepen my purpose, nurture me, and keep me proactive. And I love outside-the-box empowerment, it's the best!

S&M is chock-full of spiritual, psychological, and emotional treats. My little book is not about sexuality or erotica, it's kink-think for empowerment. Sex doesn't define S&M, and it doesn't define me-but if it frees your inner dominatrix (or submissive), that's okay too!

Since S&M was a whole 'nother world for me, I created an acronym for kink: **K**ind **I**ntent **N**urtures **K**nowing. This acronym might help you, too, as it works in both the vanilla and kink worlds. It paved the way for my dominatrix detour, which I hope empowers those who might never step a (stiletto) foot inside a dungeon.

Welcome to my journey of stepping outside of societal norms, figuring out who I would be if I granted myself freedom, and exploring all things power in BDSM. I cracked the whip so you don't have to. Here's to expressing our truth and beauty-who cares if the inspiration is unconventional? As you'll soon find, self-help can be sexy and fun!

$\mathcal{S}$ETTING THE SCENE

Don't compromise yourself.
You are all you've got. —*Janis Joplin*

Don't be too much, don't rise above, and for fuck's sake, don't swagger! All females, from girlhood to womanhood, receive these messages. We've absorbed them and, if we're really being honest, even tried to conform to them.

How about reclaiming our worth? Deep down, we want to be true to our wildest spirits and live meaningful lives. We want to own our power. Sometimes that takes TLC, and sometimes it takes a spank in the right direction.

The Little Vanilla Book is for women who want to shine. It gives "personal power" a fresh new meaning and cheers you on to live with authentic confidence. You'll be inspired to step into you, while rocking a gentle heart and sky-high stilettos.

Embracing your power is choosing not to play small. It's choosing to become your own heroine. If playing small worked, we would not need radical inspiration, but there's a time for Martha Stewart and a time for hella-real empowerment.

You're about to liberate your flawless self. How? By taking an all-new look at authenticity, self-confidence, body image, resilience, and courage. These core states show up in all aspects of your life. Each one affects whether you bring the sexy and nail life with gusto.

If you prefer homogenized inspiration, bless you, but this probably ain't the book for you. *The Little Vanilla Book* uses—*gasp*—kink-inspired wisdom for personal growth. BDSM is probably the last thing you thought would enlighten you, and I'm with you on that. But its core elements are trust, power, surrender, and self-expression.

I don't identify as kinky, and I'm assuming that you don't either if you're reading a book with "vanilla" in the title. Yet the art of domination helped me rethink my power, tenderness, and truth. My journey from vanilla to dominatrix and back delivered potent life lessons worth passing on.

Simply put, I'm vanilla with insights from the kink world. Add a big dose of humanity to those insights and you have *The*

Little Vanilla Book. This isn't about looking sexy in a corset or getting a submissive to do your housework, it's about empowering those of us—like yummy vanillas—who don't self-define as "kinky." We might have kink curiosity, but we dig in our five-inch heels when it comes to deviance.

So what is *BDSM*? It's an umbrella term for consensual erotic practices involving power play:

Bondage and **D**iscipline / **D**ominance and **S**ubmission / **S**adism and **M**asochism

All the taboos under one sexy red umbrella! "Kink" and "S&M" are shorthand.

For those about to run out and buy a latex dress and a paddle, this isn't an entrée into the kink scene. It's not even about sexuality but about your potentiality. You'll likely agree that trust, communication, personal boundaries, and honoring power and the choice of surrendering are all good principles to live by. These are the guiding principles for power play and form BDSM's "Safe, Sane, and Consensual" ethic, and are the foundation for every last spanking and handcuffing.

Seeing past BDSM taboos to kink-think can help rock your life. Everything in these pages is designed to support your calling to reach higher, embrace your divinity, live with truth, and make nice with your rockin' bod. S&M wisdom is good for the vanilla heart and soul. It may even lead to radical self-love.

Now break out those stilettos, and let's get walking.

KINK-INSPIRED VANILLA *AHA*'S

Women are not inherently passive or peaceful.
We're not inherently anything but human. —*Robin Morgan*

The biggest obstacle to women's empowerment is not living our truth. Being true to ourselves is essential and is the purest act of self-love. The opposite of that is submitting to a social script about who we're supposed to be that runs counter to what's in our hearts.

Women have gotten the message loud and clear that our looks are our primary value. Basing our value on our cheekbones, breasts, and asses does not put us in a position of power. Manifesting our truth does. Empowerment requires potent practices to not only "find" it but to constantly *bring* it. Each upcoming "life spank" is a mindful incentive to help you do just that. Each will empower you to live with swagger in spite of your supposed flaws or whether or not you got the promotion or the gold ring.

You're about to get all up in your *you*-ness (hooray!). You are going to delight in your fab self. You don't buy in to the "ideal woman" myth any more than you believe in a one-size-fits-all blueprint for life. You're about to take a step—the most important step—the first one. Mine went something like this.

I have a driving need to be of service, whether feeding the homeless or being the last resort in a crisis, and have spent time on the lines as a crisis counselor. You always get more than you give, and this was never truer than on the night I took a call from a lonely woman who just needed to talk. We chatted about life and ended up at body image (of course). The caller said she was sick of struggling with her poor body image and wanted to feel good in her skin. The maverick way she made peace with her body was by becoming a full-on nudist for a year. She'd never felt truer to herself or braver in public than trotting around in her birthday suit! Her story was hilarious and kind of profound, and it stuck with me.

My exploration of BDSM was oddly similar, minus the nudity. I chronically struggled with feeling small and unworthy (sound familiar?). My abusive childhood influenced how I showed up in life, in bad ways and good. It weighted me down like I was wearing a chainmail jacket, but it also fostered power.

I've always been drawn to matters of power—the idea of a woman unapologetically taking charge. This got me into roller derby and it compelled me to interview one dominatrix after another. I continued on to workshops and play parties at BDSM dungeons (the playgrounds for kink culture), and along the way I met eager submissives, nurturing masters, and everything in between.

Understanding the kink world changed my notions of strength. Who knew that submissives have the final word and ultimately the power? Learning this helped me redefine helplessness, just as negotiating limits schooled me on personal boundaries. But what really spoke to me was the role of domination. I discovered that I would much rather be the whip-wielding babe in latex ruling her domain rather than the facedown sub in rope bondage.

Dungeons are largely matriarchal societies. Women are revered for their strength. *Nobody* in the kink world calls a powerful woman a controlling bitch. They bow and call her Mistress. The BDSM arena is one of the few places where a woman is encouraged to be powerful and—I'll say it—*worshipped* for her strength! It is a liberating thing to witness.

Cut to my dominatrix immersion. Getting into the scene, I realized that BDSM practitioners were seriously good at communicating, setting boundaries, and fully expressing themselves. The ones I met were adventurous, high-functioning people who were having a great time getting their kink on. In fact, kinksters score better on some mental health tests than non-kinksters, having done some hard psychological work to embrace who they are, which translates to positive mental health.[1]

So I learned my way around a dungeon or three. I experienced nonsexual power exchange and consensual fetish fun. Opening up to kink created life skills that worked outside the dungeon. Giving social scripts the middle finger freed me to evolve. I showed up, kinked up, and got liberated.

Millions of kinksters see BDSM as a practical path of liberation. Surprisingly, kink-think applies to our most human concerns. It helped me realize that to rock my potential I'd have to get right with my authenticity, self-confidence, body image, resilience, and courage.

These core states shape our quality of life, and you can bet that they affect the way you love, contribute, and play. Seriously, can you name one girlfriend who hasn't struggled with confidence, courage, going the distance, or being true to herself? One woman who doesn't ever body-hate? Instead of making it a "bitches be crazy" thing, let's state the obvious: *humans* struggle. It is part of the human condition. It's hard out there for a girl (and a guy!).

The win is to learn from your struggles. My struggles created empathy, and maybe yours honed your intuition, which may have led you to this book. We draw to us what we need to learn, and life gives us endless lessons—sometimes gently, sometimes by dropping a piano onto our heads—tailored to our level of attention and openness.

Throwing our arms open to life lessons is hard and often brings up a lot of our own shit. Growth is messy. No matter what a zillion life coaches and motivational speakers say, you have to go through tough emotions to get to the other side, and that takes guts. There's nothing braver than showing up and being you, with or without your corset.

I'm here to say that showing up and getting real will serve you every time. You can learn to trust yourself and up your fun factor. You can lean into fear and get heart-naked as well as butt-naked. You can *shine*. My intention is for us to celebrate ourselves—even when it's scary and we're not feeling it, even when haters want to keep us small or when life seems too big.

For much of my life, I was hell-bent on numbing my feelings, beating myself down, and looking for fixes. I ran when people got too close. I obsessed over my "flaws," compulsively criticizing each inch of myself. I tried not to take up space because people might judge or hate me.

I sacrificed half my life to be accepted and chose a modeling career where scrutiny and rejection were constants. I battled my seesaw weight with drugs, eating disorders, and endless cardio. Eventually, the impossible notion arose that I was worth saving. One by one, I peeled away the layers of fear and self-loathing and started seeing the humanity in myself and others.

Turning my struggles into something beautiful makes me better. It gives my experiences meaning. It allows me to add my voice to the greater good. I was wounded, and I am scarred. That's okay. Scars are beautiful and make people compelling. Scars remind you of your humanity. Mostly, scars are proof that there is healing.

I used to think that my childhood trauma negatively defined me, but it made my heart tender and a champion of underdogs. It made me dig deeper and search harder. It inspired fierce workarounds that forged a warrior who's willing to fall and get up again. It connected me more deeply with my humanness.

It may seem like humanness has no place in a dungeon but it's actually an arena where personal truths are welcomed. A "dungeon" can be any safe space to explore personal power. In the kink scene, power play honors the complexity of each person. It is based on *hell-yeah!* consent. True dominants are mindful of and in tune with their partner, the emotions in the room, and the psyche in the body.

Pain and violence are also placed in a different context in a dungeon—pain is viewed as weakness leaving the body, making room for bliss. Power play takes dedication and sometimes flagellation—flogging, anyone? Long-term, 24/7, or owner-slave relationships use contracts to formally agree on aspects of power exchange. Limits, expectations, and safewords are negotiated. Yes to this, no way to that, please please *please* to another. All to lose yourself in the moment and let what is true emerge.

This was a vanilla *aha* moment for me. It wasn't just about the scene but about my personal journey. What if I paid attention to my *own* truth? What if I felt safe to explore? What if in every instance I tried to honor my deeper self? I could discover what resonated for me and let it guide my life. I could treat my well-being as contractual.

How we treat ourselves is everything. When you think about it, the truest contracts we have are with ourselves. We have to set an intention for how we'll live and love ourselves. We have to nurture this intention, because we'll get off track—it ain't a straight road, and hooray for detours. But we can make our way if we refuse to abandon our truth.

By choosing your truth you are *choosing yourself*. This is a radical act of self-love. Radical self-love is gently leaning into your heart to know and accept yourself fully. It is allowing yourself to be who you are, owning it, and saying "I am."

I encourage you to negotiate with yourself, decide how you want to play, and set rules for how you treat yourself. Seal it in a sacred contract and make sure it allows for all your humanness, whether soft and gentle or loud and proud.

Let's embrace being human. Let's give ourselves permission to fall. Let's be kinder, gentler kick-ass babes. Let's adopt Rainer Maria Rilke's motto, "Let everything happen to you. Beauty and terror. Just keep going. No feeling is final."[2] Isn't that amazing? We're fucked up and beautiful, and sometimes our jeans don't fit and our feet falter, but we can keep going. And we do.

ON AUTHENTICITY

Why fit in when you were born to stand out? —Dr. Seuss

I've done Twelve Step and box step. I've sat with swamis and motivational speakers. I dated a life coach who was so intent on remaking me that I felt like I was being run over by a bulldozer—repeatedly. His quick "fixes" didn't stick, and it never felt okay to show up as who I was in that moment. I even did a Tony Robbins fire walk! There. I said it.

While I got something from these doings, nothing made as much sense as simply rediscovering that pistol I was when I was a six-year-old. She didn't give a shit about developmental psychology or dressing Barbies because she was too busy getting her groove on. The lure of becoming that pistol again is what drove me.

When you stop trying to fit into prescribed roles, your life shifts in surprising ways. Domming was like that for me—a surprise, and yet oddly familiar. My roles as a dominatrix and a crisis counselor both put me directly in the path of people in need. Both demanded instant rapport and calm control and being trustworthy with people's truths.

I met a mogul during my domme immersion who confided that nothing felt as true to him as submitting. He felt like a fake at his power-job and with his image-based friends. He needed to give up control and serve. He came to the dungeon for pup play, a common fetish. Once our scene started, he kneeled for me to collar him and pranced around the floor on a leash, eagerly sat up, barked, and rolled over on command. *Sit! Stay! Good boy!* His eyes lit up when I treated him with puppy biscuits. I found his gratitude and joy endearing. He was clearly better off not denying this aspect of himself.

There was also a mean-as-a-snake pro domme who reveled in sadism. I saw an underlying sweetness and liked her a lot. When I asked her how she dealt with the intensity of the dungeon all the time, she looked at me curiously and said, "I'm a bitch!" She said she loved tapping into her bitchiness, and her intensity matched that of the dungeon—it was the perfect outlet for her. Both of these players found a way to be and do what felt true to them.

Domming was a way to show up and be *in* my power (and if that meant paddling a willing dude, so be it). I appreciate the eroticism of BDSM, but it's not about sex for me—and it's not always about sex for kinksters, either. Kink is about honoring power exchange.

I liked the ingenuity required for a good scene, the psychological realm, and the connection that came from a sub spilling his deepest needs (usually with his head bowed,) and reaching him at that level. And *yeah*, I like wearing a leather corset, fishnets, stilettos, and eyeliner for days. It's straight-up fun tapping into your alter ego while rocking latex.

The way we authentically express ourselves may change as we evolve. A submissive finds that he/she is a switch. A chemist finds purpose as a social worker. A lawyer finds her calling as a Broadway actor. You know your aim is true when the deepest part of you is engaged by what you're doing. Your self-expression feels honest and purposeful. If you can make that the biggest part of your life, and it serves both yourself and others, then that's spanktastic.

Latex Living

Be yourself; everyone else is already taken. —*Oscar Wilde*

An internet search for "find yourself" yields nearly 200 million results. We need a bigger lost and found! Your beauty lies in your authentic self, and the world needs more Janes—my affectionate term for females—owning their truth and rising to their potential. Directors and doctors and dancers, oh my!

There's no escaping that we're conditioned by social forces. It's human nature to internalize cultural scripts and to worry about how we measure up. It's our primal instinct to seek out love and acceptance, so we take on roles that help us fit in. Who can blame us for zigging when deep down we want to zag?

Authenticity is living your truth. It's about tapping into that pistol or punk or princess you were when you were six, before you knew there were Kardashians to keep up with. It's letting your behavior flow and owning it all—every beautiful, extraordinary, maddening layer. Owning it is a catwalk to freedom; even if that means a nip slip or stiletto tumble or two along the way. To know you is to love you!

One of the reasons I faced my fear of BDSM (what if I'm sacrificed to a dungeon god?) was to explore the way kinksters own it—showing up as puppies and sadists, baring their asses, psyches, and fetishes for all to see. They don't stifle their swerve, no matter how outrageous it may seem to us vanillas.

Self-love guru Lisa McCourt says that denying your desires is denying you. She says that once you've done the self-examination work to uncover your desires, you hurl yourself in their direction, because the universe wildly adores you and is always orchestrating on your behalf.[1] If you don't yet believe in yourself—or in an all-adoring universe—you can still manifest your truth. Start from where you're at. Get off the treadmill of outer validation and get willing to love yourself up. Create a mindful practice one spank at a time.

S&M is about being open to your leanings and accepting your kinks or jones for power play. You stroll into a dungeon, latex squeaking, and ask yourself whether you want to serve or suffer or spank (if that's your thing). You slip your shoes off and trample your eager sub. He needs the pain and humiliation and you like the feel of his body under your bare feet. Your intention is to get to the good stuff, to commit to the scene and be whoever you are in that moment.

Being authentic in the vanilla world is the same, minus the squeak . . . and the trampling. It starts with the lure of becoming. If you can fall in love with yourself just a little, if you can recall even *one* moment of pure power, soulful bliss, or self-love then you're on your way.

So how do we vanilla Janes use kink-think and S&M wisdom to accept and express our true selves?

Spank This

Fuck Up! The best first step in finding our true selves is making a deliberate decision to risk disapproval. Be willing to "fail" at being the person others accept or reject. This is often a first step on a kinkster's path to liberation. Imagine what you'd do if it didn't matter what people thought of you. Now the fun can start.

Curious Cat. A good dominatrix gets to know her subs intimately. She might jot down notes about each submissive such as, "Responds well to this, is triggered by that, revolts against this, salivates over that." Vanilla Janes can take a cue from this. Get to know what makes you tick. Tease out your leanings. Start a journal of reflections to see what rises up and wants to be expressed. Start each entry with something like, "I'm curious about my fascinating, kick-ass self!" It's a nod of approval at the outset and a permission slip to explore. The lavish attention you'll pay yourself also sends the message "I'm pretty damn interesting."

Wonder Girl. Remember the wonder you had as a kid? That's you at your core. It's simpler to reclaim that awe-filled wonder girl than you think. You know those playful things that make you giggle and do your happy dance? *Do those more.* Feed your childlike sense of wonder. Einstein said, "There are two ways to live: you can live as if nothing is a miracle, or you can live as if everything is a miracle."[2] Be that miracle.

Chisel Your Need for Approval. Getting loved up creates such a deep longing that, starting in childhood, we adapt and morph to fulfill that longing, which can result in abandoning our true selves along the way. Want to challenge your need for approval? Start *showing up* for yourself. Stand in your truth. Learn to listen to that little voice inside you. It can become your champion and warrior. Get still and quiet and breathe into it. Sit with any uncomfortable feelings that come up, and keep at it. Try on whatever arises, even if you're unsure about it—you won't know unless you give it a chance. Practice being yourself in social situations, whether a book club or a fetish club outing, by asking yourself: What's the worst that could happen? You're probably laughing about one of those worst things now. Then ask: What's the best that could happen? E. E. Cummings observed, "To be nobody but yourself—in a world that is doing its best, night and day, to make you everybody else—means to fight the hardest battle which any human being can fight; and never stop fighting."[3]

Do **You.** If you're ashamed or insecure about any aspect of yourself (physical or emotional), you'll hide those parts. That takes a lot of energy that could be better spent tying up your submissive or straddling an x-cross in anticipation of a flogging. Hiding your true self fuels the belief that you are not lovable, worthy, or acceptable. Find someone safe to come clean to, whether it's a priest, a pen pal, or a domme. Don't show the parts of you that are shiny and sexy and fun—air the stuff that you keep hidden. Unraveling your shame is a huge step toward self-acceptance. If you're not ready to show your underbelly, write your shame-secrets on a piece of paper and burn it. Let the secrets drift away with the ashes, and redefine your so-called flaws as endearing. You'll end up saying, "Hey, that's just me!" instead of, "Ugh, I'm the worst!"

Sublime Selfie. It goes without saying that self-image means a lot. We're invested in it, even if it's bad. The mental picture we have of ourselves colors our actions. Luckily, a negative self-portrait can be erased (much like deleting a selfie). It's in your power to create an image of who or what you *really* identify with. A gentle goddess? A babetastic boxer? A cultural feminist? If your self-image isn't true to your underlying vision, delete it, empty the recycle bin, and create something that you're proud of instead. Personal power comes from a strong sense of self.

Note to Self. Create a beautiful note card. Draw on it, vision-collage it, and affix a favorite photo. Write three questions on it:

What do I love?

What do I want?

What can I be?

Every morning when you wake up, read your questions aloud. *What do I love? What do I want? What can I be?* Answer these questions all day. Answer them in your laughter and your doing and your being. Write the answers on your skin where only you can see (using an organic washable marker!). Delight in the words adorning your body, and honor their invitation. When your answers become congruent with each other and your life, you're onto something. This practice will rock your world.

Self What? Most of us never got a blueprint for being kind to ourselves. Self-care was as inconceivable as unicorns. Actually it's a commitment to basic rights: rest when you're tired, eat when you're hungry, and cry when you're sad. It's being your own champion, celebrating your efforts, and soothing all the troubled places. In the S&M world, the equivalent is called "aftercare"—any type of traumatic or mentally challenging event is followed by affectionate care and attention. A domme might stroke a sub's hair while embracing them, and gently asking about their well-being. In every walk of life, things go wrong and souls get bruised when basic kindness is absent.

Killer Hipsters. Is hanging out with über cool, ironic hipsters helping you get real? Unless you're a natural, worrying about your cool factor keeps you out of the present. It keeps you from discovering whether your incentive is a fairy tale, a carrot tail, or a whip tail. Your coolness is in your authenticity, whether that shows up in how you geek out over meerkats or quantum physics or embrace your dorkiness and humanity. In *Almost Famous*, Lester Bangs (played by Philip Seymour Hoffman) says, "The only true currency in this bankrupt world is what we share with someone else when we're uncool."[4] Cool.

Check Yo' Self. This simple question will check your values: What's my motivation for doing this? You might automatically blurt, "I bake because nice girls don't arm wrestle" or "I get attention, so why rock the boat?" Jackhammer underneath that, and honor whatever you unearth. It's like being your own shrink. Kinksters know the rewards of asking the tough questions. This is like a lemon-cayenne cleanse for the soul, and it allows you to take one huge step closer to authenticity and to start choosing more honestly. Question your motivations. Question the truth of your answers. Rinse and repeat.

Wreck Yo' Self. Who told you girls are weak? Who says you can't? Wreck that shit—tear down those falsehoods and rebuild yourself better. Consider it a sadistic boot camp to force your false self to submit. This is a tough exercise in challenging notions of yourself that you're invested in. It will piss off your ego and anyone who prefers your façade, but you'll be lighter for it once you start shedding that toxic load. You'll be able to decide whether the labels you've been assigned are legit, or whether they cause you shame and need to be kicked to the curb. Get out there and make a mess! Whatever situations life throws you that stir up shame, do a mental 180 and view them as opportunities to *liberate* yourself.

Style and Substance. Are you a carefree Bohemian or an ambitious Type A? A Pollyanna or a punk? Does your wardrobe know? It does your talking when you walk into a room. It tells the world a story about you. If it reflects the you of ten years or ten pounds ago or during a bad breakup, it's time to tweak your style. Become your own image consultant (or hire one), and have fun building your style persona. Start by shopping your closet and investing in a few staples. The goal is for the image you project to express who you are. Let your clothes celebrate your true inner self. Fashion historian and costume curator Stella Blum said, "Fashion is so close in revealing a person's inner feelings, and everybody seems to hate to lay claim to vanity, so people tend to push it away. It's really too close to the quick of the soul."[5]

Wrap It Up. Rocking your innate gifts is a direct inroad to your authentic self. To reconnect with hidden talents, start a list of what you loved or were good at when you were a kid—those are your gems. Write down what you *might* be good at today. Now list all your personality traits from childhood on—no judgment! Notice which childhood traits stayed with you and which ones got squashed. Your traits and talents are your starting point to step into you. Take it from a zillion kinksters: owning who you are is therapeutic.

Kidlet. One of the many bonuses of being childlike is getting 100 percent present and real while expressing inner feelings. Oh, and it's hella fun. There was a sweet older man known affectionately as "the dungeon baby," barely over five feet and the perfect size for OTK (over the knee spanking). Having recently lost his beloved wife, he *needed* bare-bottomed spankings as release from pent up grief and loneliness. He needed to connect physically with another human by having his ass reddened. Call it catharsis or baby role-play, he kicked his feet and cried and yelped like a toddler having a tantrum. His screams shook the walls. Afterward he was blissful, having purged every last grief. He had no shame about his infantile histrionics and told me the spankings kept him going, made him feel better, and helped him articulate his true feelings. Here are some ways to connect with *your* inner kid (other than OTK):

· Skip! You can't not giggle while skipping.
· Curl up with your blankie and have a childhood movie night.
· Read a kids' book like *Green Eggs and Ham.*
· Host a game night with buddies.
· Volunteer for children's story hour at the library.
· Cry it out—kids let it all out and move on.
· Play hooky—fill out your own permission slip and have an adventure.
· Color outside the lines.
· Whip up a PB&J or other childhood meal.
· Visit a petting zoo and hug a bunny.
· Sing with abandon.

Let 'Em In. BDSM is an exercise in trust and vulnerability. Sometimes embracing who you are, both as a kinkster or vanilla, means letting people in. It's a chance to share your raw, beautiful, goofball inner self with trusted others. There's only one you, so let your freak flag fly! The people who accept your flaws and beauty now will be those you'll have history with later. Let others know who you are and that you care about them, even if you're afraid they won't reciprocate. Just stand there and swing the door open wide. Worry about swatting flies later.

Superstar You. It's safe to say that our culture is fame obsessed. Sure, the tabloids are eye candy, but what would happen if you were as fascinated by yourself as by a celebrity? Instead of sending yourself the message that you're less interesting than someone with agents and publicists, plug into your life. For every hour you spend star watching, unplug and spend two on yourself. Dance naked, meditate, create a mantra, write down ten things you dig about yourself, visit a nursing home, hug a tree, call a friend. Don't pay attention to what you *should* do but to what you *actually* do. That's your invitation to authenticity. Want to take it one step further? Set yourself on a mission that's bigger than you, whether it's getting your law degree, saving endangered lemurs, helping at-risk youth, or starting a bakery. Your mission keeps you striving and curious and ultimately fascinating.

Get Naked. Emotionally, that is. Revealing your authentic self means you might be misunderstood, rejected, or labeled. Labels are for food wrappers not people. Labeling ourselves or others based on gender, sexuality, values, or status is the opposite of acceptance and perpetuates shame. Yikes. The thing about getting naked is that you get to discover all your facets. (What else has facets? A diamond!) Being vulnerable is way harder than keeping up a façade—or is it? You may be able to leg press four hundred pounds and nail a work project while balancing a baby, but exposing your heart? Sheer terror, yet crazy rewarding. Create an intention to bare all, and you'll start to attract people who you feel free to express yourself with. These are your people! They will delight in you! If not, fuck 'em. Others will celebrate the real you. Gravitate toward them. By showing up as yourself, you'll inspire others to do the same, creating a beautiful continuum.

*You-*ness. The stronger our truth the farther our reach. So why do we deny our true selves? Maybe we don't train for the Olympics or sing at open mic night—when we're truly Olympians and songstresses—because people might laugh at us. Maybe our need to be the comic relief smothers our soulfulness. Maybe we don't explore our leanings or life purpose because of circumstances, or we're afraid that our lives will become too big if we start down that road. Maybe we were once shamed for being spectacular or sex-positive. It makes me sad to think of all the beautiful, wasted swagger in the world. In lieu of giving each one of you a hug, I will say this: You are somebody. You are supposed to be here. There has never been a person exactly like you, and there never will be again. You are the sum total of history and experience and perspective. Every moment that you express your uniqueness is a win. Every time you claim yourself and act on your *you-*ness, somewhere a dog smiles. A petal opens. Being in harmony with yourself puts you in harmony with these miracles. As author and spiritual teacher Marianne Williamson says, "Our deepest fear is not that we are inadequate. Our deepest fear is that we are powerful beyond measure."[6]

ON CONFIDENCE

A horse is a horse, of course, of course. —Mr. Ed *theme song*

I stand by the adage "how you do anything is how you do everything." My life experience wasn't in the slightest related to BDSM but informed my dominatrix experience. One surprising influence was my time spent as a cowgirl.

A good cowgirl knows one thing for sure: horses are settled by confidence. A horse can always sense when you're scared, regardless of how you try to play it off. Few things will spook a filly more than an insecure rider. You have to relax and roll with things, and the horse will follow suit. Its emotions depend heavily on the emotions of its human. And I was that human.

When I was twelve, my family moved from our Northern California 'hood to a ranch bordering Texas. I didn't know jack about ranching or riding. My first horse was a gray mare named Sirocco who ate green cowgirls for breakfast. She was built like a two-ton truck. Within seconds of getting on her back, she'd bolt and run breakneck through the woods, grunting and ducking under branches to rake me off against trees. I adored her fierce spirit, even her single-mindedness to get me the hell off her. She got my attention off myself—*Am I holding the reins right? Do I look fat in these Wranglers?*—and onto her. She upped my game, and holding my own became a source of pride.

By age fourteen, I'd learned to sling bales of hay and sacks of feed and drive pickups and tractors. I adopted an ex-racehorse nicknamed Pete, a black gelding with devilish eyes that drank me in. He was all about wind-in-your-hair, full-speed-ahead, *go*. Racing was his purpose. Stopping, not so much. When I decided to do the rodeo thing, because there weren't any malls in a fifty-mile radius, I taught Pete to pole bend and barrel race, circling the poles and barrels at a run and charging back to a sliding stop. We won our share of ribbons and trophies.

Mastering a twelve-hundred-pound racehorse spurred my confidence. I was fool-mad in love with Pete and praised him for getting things right and spent as much time letting him be *him*—madly galloping along roads and pastures—as I did coaxing him into becoming a rodeo pony. And I earned his trust by having a sure hand.

As a cowgirl, I learned that confidence matters. While I couldn't apply this wisdom to my awkward, chubby teenage self, it influences me as an adult. I try to accept people for who they are and where they're at. I've developed a sure demeanor as a workaround for my insecurities. It settles me and others.

These horse lessons snuck into the dungeon. (No, I'm not talking about pony play, although you'll find that in many a dungeon too!) A horse settled by confidence equals a submissive settled by confidence. Horses and subs require individual training to tease out their best selves. You want to gently run your hands along their body to gain their trust, communicate your intentions, be assertive, monitor their body language and emotional signals, and reward them for getting things right. It's all about a sure hand.

Horses and subs choose who to trust—you ain't the boss. Submissives have an absolute power which defies vanilla logic; horses are prey animals and will run or fight to the death if threatened. Inside each "tamed" horse or submissive is still a wild, sensitive being. It is a show of faith on their part to hand over control and consent to domination. I never took my dominant role for granted, but sought to earn it.

I think you're always communicating your confidence, whether you're a vanilla or kinkster, a cowgirl or CEO. The level of trust you inspire and the amount of control you are granted are directly related to your sure hand. Confidence makes all the difference, spurs or stilettos.

STILETTO SWAGGER

Well-behaved women seldom make history. *—Laurel Ulrich*

Stilettos are commanding. It's impossible not to power up while striking a Xena warrior pose in heels. In your stiletto height, you may be only a few inches from reaching self-love and towering confidence. But not by playing nice.

Your inner nice girl doesn't have the guts to get you there. You can't become self-actualized while you're busy being apologetic, worrying about how your hair looks, or making nice so that everyone likes you. Your inner nice girl isn't determined to shine no matter what.

Dimming your light is not why you're here. Marianne Williamson says, "Your playing small does not serve the world."[1] If only for today, let go of playing small. Instead of asking loved ones, strangers, or psychics to affirm your worth, call on your mojo. Instead of struggling for perfection, strive to own your humanness. Strive to make peace with your hair. Strive *up*.

The prevailing message is that something's missing from our lives, and that once we get it, we'll be okay. We bring the sexy and bring home the bacon but there's always something better and hotter to aim for. We live in a cult of personality and perfect tens. Fuck, sometimes don't you just want to *be*? You're enough. I'm enough. Let's love and validate our *own* selves. This is the crux of self-confidence.

Confidence is an empowering dynamic. It requires what I call a soft revolt: an inner uprising to claim your self-worth. A soft revolt is about self-love and dedication. It's about tuning out critical messages and honoring who you are. It's about—and this is a big one—accepting that you have worth by just existing as you.

If we believe that human life has value then how can we deny our *own* worth? That savage denial was once all of me. Forget confidence—I didn't believe I deserved to exist. What I've learned is that if you can make the leap of faith that you're worthwhile, it will create a shift. It's simple but life changing. *You don't have to believe it yet.* Just be willing to take the leap.

When concrete shifts even a little, flowers rise up from the cracks. What could you do if your life shifted? You could become your own heroine. You could spark your inner light. You could love yourself even when you thought you didn't deserve it—*especially* then. Because you're worth it. If I could only give you one takeaway, it would be that you profoundly matter.

Advertisers and mass media have it wrong—there's no *missing thing* that will complete us. You are a whole spiritual being. You possess the divine feminine, a creative life force at the heart of humanity. The divine feminine is the goddess in all traditions, symbolic of harmony, love, insight, and wholeness. Those are the qualities of your higher self, your heroine—whatever you want to call her. Hell, name her Ms. Sparkle Pants if it gets you there.

I don't envision a goddess as an all-knowing, bejeweled femme fatale with kohl-lined eyes. Swagger needs substance. Modesty trumps hubris. The most powerful confidence I've seen is quiet, self-assured, and contained. But really, confidence shows up differently in everyone. And, like all human states, it is not constant. You just have to own it. You have to roll with your shifting confidence by reminding yourself, "I *have* something. I *am* something. I may not be fully expressing my beauty, but I'm on my way. No one can take away my worth."

I know a feminist submissive who is all about self-worth. She *knows* she is equal to her dominant and chooses to suspend her will. Consent is sexy to her, and so is the erogenous zone of her bottom. A few sharp smacks help her connect with her feminine energy. She doesn't equate being submissive with being a victim but rather with her all-powerful choice—and if you saw her swagger, you'd agree she's got it going on.

However you rock it, you are a sacred feminine badass. It's in your DNA. You are a unique expression of the divine feminine. Make no apologies for being you. Don't justify who you are and what you want, and don't stifle your swagger. *Own* it. Go from nice girl to goddess and define yourself on your own terms.

How else can we vanilla Janes embrace our divinity and confidence?

Spank This

Wonder Woman. Power poses are Viagra for confidence. There's proof that holding a Wonder Woman pose (arms on hips, legs apart) for two minutes or more strengthens your feelings of power and confidence. It jacks up your dominance hormone and is a gateway to risk taking. Social psychologist Amy Cuddy explains that standing in a posture of confidence, even when we don't feel confident, improves how we see ourselves. Her compelling twenty-minute TED Talk illuminates how your body language shapes who you are and the likelihood that you'll succeed.[2] The next time you need to get pumped for a job interview, a dungeon party or a dinner party, strike a pose.

Act As If. Ask yourself: If you believed you were worthwhile, how would you act? What would you do? Even if it's torturous to walk across a room with your head up, do it. Woman up! When you act as if you love yourself and are worthwhile, you create the conditions for confidence to manifest in your life. This concept has become popularized as a way to attract every imaginable thing we want—from bling to Bentleys—but it's also a starting point to combat deep-held insecurities. Instead of taking a passive approach, let's *act as if* we have everything within us and around us that we need to be confident, happy, and actualized. Spoiler alert: we already do!

Power Suit. BDSM style may be seen by some as deviant, but it packs a broad cultural punch. Just look to the many female pop stars rocking edgy fetish wear. Madonna, Rihanna, Beyoncé, and Lady Gaga know what I'm talking about. Popular culture has been flirting with S&M for ages, and fetish wear offers both vanillas and kinksters an outlet for power dressing. As a dominatrix, my mental state was hot-wired by dressing in a catsuit, corset, and thigh-high boots. It was a uniform that screamed power. The equivalent is the office power suit or a pair of yummy jeans that remind you you're *all that*. Fashion enhances your state and makes a statement. Win-win.

Lighten Up. There's a reason many names for BDSM practices end in "play." There is a life force that exists within play—if we approach things as fun it helps us evolve. So if you're taking yourself too seriously, then play! A sense of humor puts insecurities into perspective. Regularly ask yourself what you want to do for fun—fun for its own sake, not something squeezed between dilemmas or work projects. Let your subconscious work on all those pesky issues while your inner kid plays. Strap on old-school roller skates and hit the rink, or go to an outdoor movie-picnic-music event. Take a sitcom meal break or do a happy dance. Milk-spewing hilarity is good for whatever ails you.

Gifted. Everyone in our world of seven billion people is good at something, so start by discovering your one thing. Even if it's applying lipstick with your breasts like Claire in *The Breakfast Club*, own that shit. Pick something small and take action—every little thing you master is a win. Learning to crochet? Check. Learning to belay up a fifty-foot cliff? Check. Learning to master a bullwhip? Check. If you're seeing a pattern here, you're right. Confidence is based on action, and doing things well sends a huge message to your brain that you are an assured, capable person.

Vanilla Goddess. If it's good enough for Jennifer Aniston, it's good enough for me. The actor shares, "You know when I feel inwardly beautiful? When I am with my girlfriends and we are having a goddess circle."[3] Goddess circles are healing, transformative places to share with other women. Don't get thrown by the term "goddess"—it's symbolic of our innate divinity, strength, and wisdom. In a typical gathering, women sit in a circle and create an intention to work toward, such as releasing negativity, and they practice heart-based sharing. They may take turns leading the group to share their perspectives, and a group theme often emerges. The idea is that the whole is greater than the sum of its parts. Sister power!

Brainy Jane. Like, duh, we all know that reading makes us sexy-smart. Reading broadens our worldview and enriches our inner life, transforming us from the inside out. What you may not know is how it increases your emotional intelligence. Dommes rock emotional intelligence through empathy and awareness, while subs are good at listening and mastering their emotions. Kinksters I've met are self-aware and into reading, whether erotica, novels, or BDSM contracts! Reading novels makes us all better at our jobs and relationships, because it boosts our accurate awareness of ourselves and others.[4] Identifying with fictional peeps helps us feel less alone, and understand ourselves and friends more deeply—you're building people skills while devouring prose. Books are humanity on the page! So start a goddess reading group. Choose books that empower feminine energy, and discuss them with gal pals. Using the format of a goddess circle, gather round in your sexy-smart specs!

Rock Your Body. The vast majority of our "talking" is done through our tone of voice, facial expressions, and body language. Creating confident mannerisms translates into *actual* self-confidence, so make the most of your nonverbal communication. Dommes demand respect, obedience, and worship through their inherent being. Their body language says "I'm a boss ass bitch," which sets the stage. From the domme's bag of being:

· Hold eye contact and smile (playfully, openly, maleficently).
· Relax your shoulders or wherever you hold tension.
· Carry yourself with queenly command—walk with intent and take yo' damn time.
· Don't spend your energy on people who don't give you their full attention and respect. If you're not treated with reverence, refuse to play.

- If you're not sure what to do in a scenario, get curious—curiosity is sexy and will keep the energy flowing.
- Use fear or uncertainty (yours or another's) as a cue to pull yourself up to your full height. If that doesn't work, strike a Wonder Woman pose and think, "I've got this."

Talk Pretty. Verbal confidence means clearly expressing your thoughts, feelings, and needs, and not devaluing your message with uncertainty and negativity. Just clearly and kindly say what's true for you. Good subs are excellent listeners and their messages are well thought out (and they turn up the communication skills when uncollared). Bad subs speak when not spoken to—unless they're shouting their safeword! Good dommes are skilled in clarity and directness. Bad dommes scream and rely on histrionics ("I SAID KNEEL!"). From the domme's bag of gab:

- Pause before speaking to shape your ideas. Don't rush your thoughts.
- Speak with an assured tone, whether it's sensual, instructive, or scolding.
- Empathize with your listener to reach them where they're at.
- Watch their eyes. The eyes don't lie and will inform your message.
- Notice their body language to know when you've gotten through and ask them to paraphrase your message to see if it landed.

- Learn to say no and handle conflict.
- Seek to fully understand (in the kink world, misunderstood intent spells disaster). Be mindful and present by devoting your full attention, which will pave the way for speaking your truth.
- Get curious and ask questions. Always practice the kink world's number-one rule: be open-minded!

Talk Dirty. I adore language—the sexy sway of lyricism, the clever shuffle of satire. I love ballistic verse and juicy metaphor, and fucking hell do I love expletives. Everyone knows that dropping the F-bomb brings a point home like no other. Johnny Carson once said that you should never use a big word when a dirty little one would do.[5] Even my saintly mother said "damn" every three months or so. Swearing well is an art that includes knowing when not to swear (like around kids or swamis). Rocking a well-rounded vocabulary allows you to express what filthy words cannot. Being able to speak with people where they're at—whatever their vocabulary or ideology—is a shot of pure empathy for your fellow man. Being well-spoken allows you to verbalize your deepest feelings, opinions, and worldview—and it's free, courtesy of your local library. The point is to fully express your beautiful mind and heart. Reach right in and give us what you got, whether in song or poem or fuckery-laden philosophy. Find the balance between making an elegant point and cussing like a sailor on leave.

Demystify Swagger. In *The Charisma Myth*, Olivia Fox Cabane explains that charisma is a set of learned behaviors—Marilyn Monroe could turn hers on and off like flipping a switch.[6] If you don't feel you've got that extra somethin' somethin', you just have to learn to produce charismatic behaviors. Charismatic people seem to have power and extraordinary "presence," and they seem to like you a lot. From Oprah to Amy Schumer, culture queens and dommes, they all work their charisma and you can too. Projecting that rare combination of strength and warmth can be practiced and polished.

Lioness Pride. This is going to be hard but simple. Ready? Give yourself permission to take pride in your strengths. In fact, list those bad boys! This is no time to be humble—list every single thing you're good at and the traits you love about yourself. Are you good at taking direction or taking control? At persuasion or submission? At playing well with others? (All traits of kinksters.) It's a powerful tool to keep these positive messages around. The reminders will pave the way to becoming comfortable with who you are despite the opinions of others, which is a chief quality of a truly confident, not-faking-it Jane.

Prevent PMS. Staying stuck in fuckups amounts to handcuffing yourself to the past. It saps your will to reinvent yourself and fine-tune a beautiful you. Past Mistakes Syndrome (PMS) sabotages your stroll. For one day, give yourself permission to uncuff and start fresh. Forgive yourself for every supposed mistake. If you believed that life events unfolded when and how they were meant to, how would you show up today? Wouldn't it be great if you surprised yourself?

Whip Negativity. Negative thoughts are the critical inner voices that keep you down. Everyone has them. Anytime you catch a shitty thought before it has a chance to make you feel bad is a win. So is gently acknowledging rather than suppressing it. Love yourself in spite of your toxic thoughts. Once you are conscious of habitual thoughts, you can challenge their validity. Author Byron Katie's *Loving What Is* teaches you to challenge thoughts by asking, "Is it true? Can I absolutely know it's true? How do I react when I believe that thought? Who would I be without the thought?"[7] This allows your mind to seek the answers that lie beneath what you think you know. It provides a space to stop tearing yourself down, love yourself up, and insert kindness. Cultivate positive thoughts as part of self-care. As *Saturday Night Live* self-help guru character Stuart Smalley would say, "I'm good enough, I'm smart enough, and doggone it, people like me!"[8]

Kinky Boots. Subs and nature lovers know the power of being grounded through mindfulness (or bare feet), while dommes know that you can heighten your command with heels. Stilettos are essential to the makeup of a dominatrix, raising her above her submissive and illustrating her power. Even when other props fail, heels can do wonders for confidence and posture. Learn to walk in stilettos by using a grocery store cart for balance while trolling the aisles, extending a straight leg with each step. Whiplash on aisle five!

Mighty Aphrodite. While our alpha traits are essential, our strength lies in our wondrous femininity, our sensual core. Our female qualities of softness, grace, and compassion balance our male qualities. It's good to have both; that's what makes the world go round. Being in our feminine power means living authentically and speaking our truth without apology in only the graceful, knowing way that women can. Go deep for your truth and give thanks for your fierce spirit and sensual core. Whether you identify with Athena, Mother Teresa, Joan of Arc, or Joan Jett, you can honor the feminine as sacred. How lucky are we as women to possess the divine feminine?! We are harmony, wisdom, love, healing, and creativity. Take some time to get your head around *that*.

On Body Image

> Freedom from obsession is not something you do;
> it's about knowing who you are. —*Geneen Roth*

Our body confidence is regularly put to the test. Working out around hard-bodies can zero us in on jiggly underarms or dimpled thighs. Dating can bring up insecurities about our hotness. Glancing at photoshopped magazine covers can skid us down the road of comparison. Trying on bikinis in dressing room mirrors can wreck our mood—would it kill those sadists to give us flattering light? Come on!

Perfection pressure afflicts all Janes, and it really messed with my head as a model. Models aren't the mavens of confidence you'd think. The constant scrutiny and pressure to be perfect is like sucking in your gut 24/7 without a break. Being dismissed or glorified depending on the day is soul bruising. To survive intact, you need to be really gentle and balanced and forgiving of your flaws, which I wasn't. If I'd already taken my dominatrix detour, I would have had more body confidence, healthier boundaries, and known how to own the room. But I was a mess in my twenties, like a lot of us. Modeling was hell on my body image. I starved and binged and purged and drugged and pummeled my body into shape. I didn't have the skills to rock a modeling career *and* a healthy mindset.

Don't get me wrong; there was a lot of good. There was the cover shoot in the Maldives, the frolicking in Australia, the ad campaigns from London to Chicago. There was the Revlon contract and—I'll say it—slumming with celebrities. Sometimes I got out of my own way, had a blast, and even got my swagger on. Modeling afforded me *such* independence. I got to be a nomad and a fuckup and a somebody all at once.

And yet I also felt powerless and not in a "isn't it fun to be spanked?" sort of way. Fashion trends, body types, and hair color were deciding factors in whether I was going to work. In Italy, I was yelled at for refusing to take my top off for photo shoots. In Paris, my agent freaked out that I was twenty years old and ordered me to say I was sixteen. I lost jobs when my weight seesawed and, worst of all, my eating disorder began to run riot.

Long before modeling, I started a war against what I now see as cute preteen pudginess. The sad reality is that most girls start developing shitty body images at a young age. By middle school we're often cutting calories. In high school I took up appetite suppressants and dieting—my gateways to hard drugs and bulimia. Modeling didn't cause my eating disorder—it exacerbated it. My story is a darker, more extreme example of what happens to women on a (usually) subtler scale and a reminder to be gentle, balanced, and forgiving of yourself.

Supermodel Cameron Russell nails it in her bold TED Talk: "Models have the thinnest thighs and the shiniest hair and the coolest clothes, and they're the most physically insecure women probably on the planet."[1] In my search to find meaning beyond the land of thin thighs, I found my way to Roller Derby. I geeked out from the sidelines, awed by the way rollergirls laid down kickass while rocking every size and shape of body, and even every hair color on the spectrum. (This athletic breed of power-babe would become my gateway to BDSM's breed of power-babe, as you'll find.)

A roller derby bout is more fun than a fashion show. It's glittered and tattooed rollergirls thundering down a track in fishnets and booty shorts, and more. It's a strategic sport with a high level of athleticism and a huge skillset. It's a tits-in, all-derbs-all-the-time, contact sport with plenty of hits, blocks, and falls. Physical prowess and attitude are mandatory, plus you get to have a cool name! All of that spoke to me and I realized that my body, if I wanted it to, could hold a sort of strength that wasn't being pedestalled by the modeling industry and pop culture.

So even before I opted out of my two decades of modeling, I started training to become a rollergirl. My love of all things derby trumped the fact that I'd never played a sport (and couldn't skate). It was one of the hardest things I'd ever done, both mentally and physically, and also the raddest. I had to add muscle and functionality to my battered body. I couldn't get athlete-strong as a skinny-fat sugar junkie, so after a lifetime of cheesecake, chocolate, ice cream, cookies, and Jelly Bellys— *so* many Jelly Bellys—I went cold turkey. I ate frequent, high-protein meals dense in nutrients. I weight trained like a mother.

In six months, it was good-bye Olive Oyl, hello muscle tone! I went from skinny-fat to my fittest ever. I took immense pride in eating and training like an athlete, with grueling roller derby practices several times a week. I loved that my body could now do cool derby moves like juking and jamming and giving whips and booty blocks. I felt better in my skin.

Somewhere along the line, my craving for strength and self-actualization had an unexpected side effect. It diminished my body hate. I stopped obsessing over my flaws and ripping every inch of my body to shreds. I steered my attention from how I looked to what I was capable of. It was a radical shift in focus. I'm not saying I'm always 100 percent at ease in my skin—that's crazy talk. Self-love is a lifelong gig.

Redefining my ability was a spank in the right direction. Being gentler and less critical felt weird and uncomfortable at first, but I kept at it. The day came when I set an intention to be kind to myself no matter what. It was so much bigger than me that I didn't realize I was reinventing myself. After thousands of failed attempts, I overcame the devastating eating disorder I'd had since I was sixteen. It felt like I'd been spared by divine intervention, and the lifted burden deepened my gratitude and awareness.

Through all this I learned that grace exists. That being capable is more empowering than being skinny. That every woman has shit to work through about the way she looks. That you come equipped with an inner heroine and an inner athlete. That chasing outer validation will bite you on the ass. That becoming fit can help you to love the skin you're in. And that radical openness can change your life.

Which takes us back to how roller derby was my gateway to BDSM. There are crazy similarities between the worlds of derby and kink. Derby is a contact sport played by skilled, badass babes using force; domming is a "contact sport" played by skilled, badass babes using force. Derby and kink are both highly body-positive. Both are theaters of spectacle. Both flaunt edgy style: fishnets, latex and leather, booty shorts, duct-taped nipples, spandex, and girly skirts. And both could be said to eroticize pain! So the leap from one to the next was not huge for me.

The fashion, derby, and kink worlds all have elements of erotica, artistry, and pageant. In the theater of the dungeon, body shapes and sizes drop away in service of self-expression and exploration. A dominatrix is valued for her competency and what she brings to the table (or spanking bench, bondage horse, or X-cross). While body positivity starts inside, I highly encourage Janes from all walks of life to find that place where her body is prized or at least accepted. Sequin pasties and fishnets optional.

BREAKING BONDAGE

There is no wrong way to have a body. —*Glenn Marla*

Body image is defined as "a subjective picture of one's own physical appearance established both by self-observation and by noting the reactions of others."[2] (Thanks, library!) This picture of our physical selves is often sadly distorted.

If you want to know why women have fucked-up body images, blame the media. Or the culture-wide sexualization of girls and women. Or the invention of scales and mirrors. To start the healing process is to stop separating our body image from our relationship with ourselves.

Placing blame isn't owning what's in our control, which is the way we relate to ourselves. It's not possible to connect to our hearts while objectifying our bodies. Not treating our bodies as projects or as our primary value allows us the space to redefine our self-image. We can begin to accept our bodies by radically loving ourselves.

Radical self-love is, well, radical. It's not just shit that "crunchy mamas" talk about—it drives how you live your whole life. It's looking beyond your scars to your spirit. It's embracing your awkwardness and epic fails, your divinity and wholeness, and your magnificent bod. It's being your own best friend who sees your worth beyond size and sex appeal.

What if you were happy—not just happy, but *ecstatic*—in your own skin? Could this be a perk of radical love? What if radical love were engraved on the heart of every human in the world? It would surely put pants size into perspective.

Almost all women, from anorexics to athletes, struggle with body image. Body loathing has become so prevalent that it's almost a given in the female experience. We all know what it feels like to hate the bodies we live in to different extents, and body hatred has as much to do with how we relate to ourselves as it has to do with cultural oppression.

How we think about ourselves and talk to ourselves has a powerful effect on our identity. Author and activist Anne Lamott says, "I am not my cellulite. At fifty-nine, I finally love my strong, jiggly thighs. They just happen to be a part of the package, which is so gorgeous and juicy that a swimsuit can scarcely contain it."[3] Can you imagine saying something so radical? Let's try!

Start noticing your obsessive body thoughts (wanting to be thinner, curvier, taller, shorter, lighter, darker, smoother, *other*). Decide if all that mental energy is worth it. Decide whether you're more fulfilled by a life of connection and passion and awareness, or the pursuit of the perfect body.

Move in to your body. Savor and forgive it. Protect and listen to it. Be vigilant about what feels safe and unsafe. Notice what creates power or passiveness or bliss.

In S&M the body becomes a vehicle for pleasure and pain, but it's also a vehicle for awakening. Tools such as whips, sensory deprivation, and binding are often used to concentrate and tune the mind to the body. This tuning creates a grounding in the now, like each swat of a spanking bringing the mind inward as it focuses on first the sting and then the blood-rushing heat and then the rush of endorphins. When the senses are allowed to lead, our experiences become intuitive.

This body awareness can get lost in the vanilla experience, instead of being integral to it. Instead of enquiring within ourselves, we ignore our inner voice. Rather than embodying our innate divinity, we numb our feelings with food, drugs, or alcohol. We are driven by logic and schedules instead of openness and instincts. But our connection with spirit and wellness—even our swagger—depends on getting deeply in touch with ourselves.

Trusting our intuition and acting on it takes courage. So does being open to that which is beyond the physical dimension. These are things that kinksters are very, very good at. Like practitioners of BDSM, we should all remember that our bodies are deep truth-tellers. "Ouch" or "Yum" gets the point across when logic fails.

"There is no wrong way to have a body." Doesn't that say it all? I'd add that there's no right way to have or *hate* a body at all.

So how do we vanilla Janes make peace with our rockin' bods?

Spank This

Your Body Knows. Eat when you're hungry. Rest when you're tired. Laugh out loud. Unplug and get out into nature. Get all up in there—hug a tree, sink your toes into the grass, tilt your face up to the sun. It will nourish your body and spirit better than Oreos. Once you learn to nuture yourself, you can turn that care toward others, just like giving aftercare to a submissive! Or there's always shoulder rubs!

Body of Poetry. Write a love letter to your body. Apologize to the parts you loathe, and praise the parts you like. We all like something about our bodies. Usually it's a part that allows you to experience a joyful aspect of life. Maybe it's your hands, because you love to play the piano. Maybe it's your legs, because you love to run. The goal is to acknowledge and love up all of you. The love letter can be on scented stationery, or it can be written directly onto your delicious skin. Break out those organic washable markers and tattoo yourself with poetry.

Fine Tuning. The natural sensitivity and wisdom of our bodies gets buried under accumulated conditioning, disconnection, and even trauma. That's how we lose our mojo. We live in our heads more than we sense our bodies, but we can reconnect to our inner wisdom. In BDSM power play, the stakes are raised for your sensitivity to pain (and pleasure). Intuition is paramount—you have to trust your instincts about who is safe to play with and to entrust with your psyche and body. Attuning to your body's wisdom takes patience, willingness, and letting your heart lead. Start by engaging your senses: take a moment to really notice your surroundings, savor food, hear music, and feel your breath. Notice how your body feels in this moment without thinking about it. Just get still and aim for one second of becoming pure sensation. This practice of mindfulness—a state of openness, awareness, and focus—will deepen over time and enable you to discover your deeper truths. You'll get better at listening to your instincts and letting your inner compass guide you. Mindfulness can bring up some tough emotions but allows us to wake up to our authentic experiences.

Seussville. Did you know that Dr. Seuss wrote a book for adults about naked women heroes? No joke! *The Seven Lady Godivas* is a subversive satire on the ancient legend. Each of the Godivas are illustrated as innocent "sheros" with different shapes, sizes, and ages, exemplifying the body positivity that rollergirls, dommes, and feminists rock today. Each Godiva gains wisdom from a scruffy, charming horse and shares her truth with her naked troupe. Oddly awesome female empowerment and a reminder that life lessons can come in unlikely packages.

Love Brigade. Bondage in BDSM is consensual and fun. Mental bondage, not so much. Eleanor Roosevelt said, "No one can make you feel inferior without your consent."[4] Refuse to be dehumanized. Dehumanization can occur during groupthink, bullying, assault, predatory violence, microaggression, or objectification. The end result is that if oppression succeeds, we feel less than human. When women are objectified, we are reduced to our bodies. You are not your body. You are not an object. You are love incarnate. You cannot control everything that happens to you, but you can control your perspective about it. Refuse to let the fuckers win, and no matter what wrong is done to you, fight to believe that you are still a worthwhile human being. This point of view may take a while—it's taken me my whole life. Let's stand up for each other when we see a wrong and love up our universal family.

Mind Body Spirit. Living a holistic lifestyle means caring for all your parts from head to soul. It's living your life in a way that is natural to you and the world in which you live. Holistic wellness integrates your emotional, mental, spiritual, and physical aspects, which are the very aspects that come into play (pun!) in BDSM. A holistic lifestyle includes practicing awareness and positive action, respecting yourself and others, nurturing your spirit and conditioning your body, and adopting peaceful practices such as yoga and meditation. I'm not going to get all hippie on you—pick up a book about holistic living and bite off what you can. It will quell the impulse to look like a Barbie, if for no other reason than the toxic plastic.

Sit With It. Here's a do-nothing exercise that will have you sweating. To combat your preoccupation with minor or imaginary body flaws, set a timer for one minute and sit with the negative thoughts. This removes the knee-jerk habit of responding with avoidant and compulsive behaviors. Just sit there instead of getting on the scale or searching for your floral Mumu or reaching for the chips because you're "fat" anyway. For this one minute, don't do anything. Just accept the presence of yucky feelings and distorted thoughts. Think of them as clouds passing over you. The point is to learn to observe and release the thoughts without them triggering negative emotions. Learning to stay neutral and to let go is part of emotional balance.

Dear Jane. Journaling is like holding a thoughtful conversation with your higher self. By writing down your thoughts, you'll gain insight into your inner workings, which promotes growth, catharsis, and acceptance. Journaling can help you process your journey through joy, pain, power, and surrender. It can even help repair your broken relationship with your body. All you need is a pen and a pad of paper. Start from where you are without censoring your thoughts or editing your feelings. Embrace it all.

Goddess Worship. A staple of the kink world is body worship, or physically revering a part of another person's body. Body worship is usually an erotic fetish and often an act of submission. Having my feet worshipped by a sub helped me honor them too. Foot fetishists seriously love to pamper feet, and why not? Your feet have walked the earth in search of enlightenment, and they deserve praise. Vanilla examples of body reverence could be lavishing your love-starved parts with cream, getting a massage, or finding that person with a fetish for the very body part you want to make up with. Hugs all around!

Soul Food. *Women, Food, and God* is a lovely book by Geneen Roth that empowers women to become intuitive eaters rather than emotional eaters. Roth's view is that giving ourselves permission to eat what we want heals our food obsessions. I believe this is a starting point on your path to freedom. Roth's books have informed my healing, and this one covers our relationship with food and spirituality:

> It's never been true, not anywhere at any time, that the value of a soul, of a human spirit, is dependent on a number on a scale. We are unrepeatable beings of light

and space and water who need these physical vehicles to get around. When we start defining ourselves by that which can be measured or weighed, something deep within us rebels.[5]

Body Talk. Consider joining a women's group to heal body image issues and share in community. (Less like Weight Watchers and more like a "body worship" BDSM workshop.) Supporting each other is a huge step toward more love and awareness, and less Jane-on-Jane hate. In a supportive environment, we can express ourselves about important issues and connect with others in a meaningful way. Encouragement from other women is key in daring to shine. Supporting one another is a neglected source of strength, and bare-hearted relationships are central to joyful journeys. Sisterhood is healing.

Film Femmes. Get inspired by movie heroines. While there are a lot of lame, sexist portrayals of women in media, there are also progressive portrayals. There's Sandra Bullock in *Gravity*, Jennifer Lawrence in *The Hunger Games*, and Shailene Woodley in *The Fault in Our Stars*—"sheros" who are humble, reflective, and fierce. There's the indomitable Rebel Wilson in *Pitch Perfect*, Monica Bellucci in *Malèna*, Gabourey Sidibe in *Precious*, Julia Roberts in *Erin Brockovich*, and Jessica Lange in, well, anything. Perhaps the fiercest action heroine of all time, who triumphs as a compassionate warrior and guardian of women, is Charlize

Theron's "Imperator Furiosa" in *Mad Max: Fury Road*. When thrilling heroines like Furiosa are humanized rather than sexualized, and own their journey rather than helplessly ride sidecar, it creates a dialogue about feminine power that serves us all. Host a heroine film night to celebrate badass babes.

Don't Hate, Celebrate. Accept that bodies come in a variety of shapes and sizes, contrary to what the media would have us believe. This variety is what makes us interesting! Celebrating your curvy, thin, and in-between sisters will make it easier to celebrate yourself. As S&M pinup girl Bettie Page used to say, "I love to swim in the nude and roam around the house in the nude. You're just as free as a bird!" Fuck the myth of the "perfect" body. You remember Anne Lamott, the author and activist who loves her thighs? She says that perfectionism is the voice of the oppressor.[6] She's right.

True Jeans. Bodies have weekly and monthly changes in weight and shape—your weight can fluctuate a few pounds in a single day. Weighing yourself constantly puts too much focus in the wrong place—who cares? Don't weigh! The important thing is to have comfortable clothes that fit you at each beautiful, fluctuating stage. One of my favorite things about rollergirls, dommes, and all variety of kinksters was the audacious defiance with which they presented their bodies, not letting a little bloat or cellulite (or even doubters) wreck their roll. Accepting your body's variance allows you to get on with the business of joy and flaunt your sexiest curve—your smile.

Get Primal. I'm a carnivore. I have more vitality and am satiated by grass-fed beef, and my body craves it. And you certainly can't last through a night of play in a dungeon on a diet of lettuce and carrots! I won't argue for the health benefits of eating red meat because nutrition is individual and body chemistries vary. But whole foods from the earth and primal eating is good for every body. Go ahead. Cook a filet mignon medium rare, pick that bad boy up with your hands, and tear in. Me, Jane.

Mirror Retraining. Notice where your eyes go when you pass a mirror. Do you selectively focus on your "flaws" instead of taking in the whole picture? Is your vice checking for stomach bloat and criticizing yourself? Trade this disempowering habit for kindness. Stand in front of a mirror in clothes that show your shape. Instead of focusing on your flaws, describe yourself in neutral terms like "I have long hair. I'm wearing a blue shirt." Now describe yourself in positive terms like "I'm having a fant-abulous hair day. This blue shirt brings out my dazzling eyes." Make this a habit and follow Dita Von Teese's advice: "I make it a point to never, ever point out my physical flaws . . . this is advice I give to women as often as I can."

Move Your Body. Enough said.

Move Your Spirit. Never enough said.

Lift This. Women should lift weights. Resistance training—using bodyweight, bands, free weights, or machines—is essential. It revs up your metabolism, burns fat, strengthens your bones, creates curves and muscle tone, amps your confidence, zaps depression, and is a gateway to athleticism. Oh, and it makes you feel like a badass. Money can't buy the feeling of badassery that lifting gives, but money *can* buy one session with a sports trainer to learn a routine and correct form.

Body Paint. You thought art therapy was just for little Janes? Think again. It's a legit outlet for expressing your creativity and feelings. Art making is widely practiced in wellness and crisis centers (and eating disorder clinics) for Janes of all ages. Being creative is a natural expression of being feminine and heals the soul. Become your own art therapist and start making stuff. Let your inner Jane be your guide around the art supply store, indulging in texture and color and different mediums, and then set her loose. Consider painting yourself (or another special someone) in glorious hues of skin friendly paint. The benefits of artistic self-expression include reflection, happiness, and personal growth. Oh, and a vacation from body obsession.

Mahalo. Gracias. Merci. Your body is more than just the thing that gets you around. Whether tasting the frosting you just whipped up or getting whipped yourself, your body is the vehicle through which you experience all shades of life. Cool, huh? Here's a mindfulness exercise to stoke your gratitude and kiss your body better. The next time you have a critical body thought, counter it by celebrating one of the amazing things your body does for you. It's okay to relearn this lesson often. Rather than judge yourself, neutralize your mental diss by asking, "What cool things can my body do? Run a marathon? Hug a dog? Play Chopin? Thanks, body!"

The Simple Pleasures. Vedanta is a modern form of Hinduism.[7] Occasionally I go to Vedanta services, as nonjudgmental, all-inclusive Eastern philosophies resonate with me. After the teachings, some of us hang out and eat lunch with the swami, which is a delight. The swami is a profound dude who drops a lot of wisdom. He tells jokes—*good* ones—and references Carl Jung, dream analysis, and Eckhart Tolle. But I won't soon forget the look of bliss that crosses his face when a succulent plate of vegetarian curry is placed in front of him. Just saying.

On Resilience

Wheresover you go, go with all your heart. —*Confucius*

I never got why anybody in their right mind would want to be vulnerable. I couldn't get why a sub would choose to be "weak." I like being strong. Strong means being able to stay the course, survive what life throws at you, and be a force. While I craved safekeeping, I've had to be lionhearted from a young age. Bendy softness? Ew!

Strength is to resilience what vulnerability is to weakness. Or so I thought. Now I think the most badass battle cry is "I'm Gumby, dammit!" Yeah, that's right, Gumby. The bendy green humanoid with a faithful pal named Pokey. Gumby's plucky spirit and especially his *flexibility*—literally and figuratively—help him overcome his nemeses, which is kind of a great lesson when you think about it.

Gumby's lessons were lost on me as a little kid. I was in full-on survival mode by the time I was six, thanks to a merciless stepdad. I learned to hide my sweet little heart and disappear. I lost my mojo. It's a little-known fact that Edvard Munch painted *The Scream* while shacking up at my house.

Fuck that noise.

I decided I would never be weak again. No one would see my sensitivity or need for love. I glorified the three Bs of traditionally male traits: boldness, bravado, and balls. I donned my Wonder Woman cape and boots and walked hard. Girl power! Women warriors!

It was a hard left turn from pain and the best I could do, given my fucked-up blueprint. My childhood lesson about limits was bravely saying *no* to abuse. It proved that I could stand strong against anything. It deepened my resolve to never be broken. But it also cemented my near-phobic fear of helplessness.

My response to helplessness was to control. I was terrified if I let go of any detail of my life, the world I was shouldering would crash to bits. I tried to control my *body* with bulimia, my *feelings* with numbing drugs, my *fear* with fight or flight (enabled by my nomadic modeling career). I was enslaved by my perfectionistic, relentless need for control.

I even tried to control fate. When my mother got sick I rushed in to save the day. I stomped around and made a ruckus and handled shit. Fuck brain tumors, my beloved would be fine! In the end, all my well-intended efforts did not fix or heal or save her. Letting go of control and comforting her, *really* being present for her, would have been the greatest gift.

I wish I'd known when my mother was alive that letting go is the answer. It is the everything, the life breath, the now. I needed to let go of who I thought she should be and how she should mother me. I needed to let go of my fury against her illness because it hindered our closeness. I needed to let go of my panic over becoming an orphan. But I raged and gripped harder.

Sometimes the toughest thing for women is surrendering control. Whether you're a boss lady, mommy, or feminist, letting go can be daunting. There's always the "see, I told you shit would fall apart!" validation that you *do*, in fact, carry the world on your shoulders.

It took me years to honor my softness and sensitivity. And I'm stronger for it. I'll always be learning to let go. I'll always be fine-tuning and rebalancing. It took leaning hard into my so-called power to find my center and practicing as a dominatrix—bondage cuffs, collars, floggers, and all—was part of finding my center. I needed to experience unapologetic power and reclaim my mojo. I needed to figure out boundaries. I *thought* I needed to crush helplessness, once and for all—when I really just needed to redefine it. "Helpless" submissives showed me the strength of being present and accepting what *is*. They taught me to *cooperate* with surrender.

It's ironic that it took a submissive to teach me the value of letting go. And not just any submissive. For me, it took a raging alpha sub. For about a year, my gym buddy was a beast of a bodybuilder named Vince. I like to hold my own with alpha dudes, and we had fun talking smack while lifting. Vince had given me his number and kept telling me to call him, but I wasn't having it. I wasn't interested in dating The Hulk or ending our smack talk. But early into my dominatrix detour, he invited me to a dungeon party. He swore afterward that he didn't know I'd be down, but that my gym vibe seemed different.

The night of the play party, we mingled at the fetish club with some flirty leather and latex kinksters, while a collared sub sat at his mistress's feet, and a guy with full-sleeve tats and a bull-ring chatted up a domme in a schoolgirl skirt and bustier. Vince and I were understated—I wore a little black dress, leather cuff, and stilettos; Vince wore jeans, a crisp shirt, and dress shoes. There was a spread of food from guac and chips to chicken curry and nonalcoholic cider. It was like a (deviant) family gathering. Finally I turned to Vince and said, "So what gives?"

He grinned and told me that barbarity was too easy. He won bodybuilding competitions because he was a pain slut. He said he could withstand any amount of pain when he trained at the gym, because he could withstand it in the dungeon—he was a hardcore submissive. He joked that surrender made him superhuman like Popeye's spinach. Over the course of the next hour, part of which he spent crouched in a cage, with me holding his leash in one hand and the cage key in the other, he broke every "rule" of strength and weakness, and broke my brain in the best way. He explained how freeing himself of decisions and control recharged his energy, cleared his head, and balanced him. And *that*, he said, was why he crushed all the other bodybuilders in competitions.

Submissives exemplify the value of being where your feet are, letting go, and saying, "here is my limit, I can stretch no further" and bouncing back into form (like green Gumby clay or green Hulks). Discovering your limits is an act of self-love. So is evolving past them. Your surrender, your limits, and your lionhearted bravery are all the stuff of resilience.

I've proven my force. I can withstand anything. I've raged and grieved and hated. I've stood in kindness and grace. What I know is that I value my tender heart above all.

HARD LIMITS

> Once we accept our limits, we go beyond them.
> —*Albert Einstein*

We are happiest when we're striving toward our full potential. This is our great calling. Even the universe calls us upward with its pull of becoming. Striving toward our potential helps us find meaning and makes us solid.

When we're solid in ourselves, we stand strong. We are resilient. Resilience is having grit and not letting hardship or epic struggles define you. It allows you to come back stronger after getting knocked down—like taking a roller derby hit and charging on again.

The marrow of resilience is knowing in your very core that you won't give up, no matter what. This inner knowing trumps any outer circumstance. Your inner voice is like the friend who tells you there's spinach in your teeth or the coach who gives you tough love. It's your truth.

You already have what you need inside. Keep listening to your inner voice, and your life will roll forward with meaning. You've got this. Use everything else—the reminders of love, strength, and compassion—to reconnect with that inner knowing. Whatever resonates can help guide you.

It helps to know what motivates you and keeps you positive. It helps to trust that you will stick up for yourself in every situation, and that you can depend on yourself to stand strong (or let go). It helps to have mindful incentives. That's what the life spank practices are for—they help you champion yourself and take the hits. They'll cheer your inner heroine.

Woven within these pages are key elements of resilience: self-confidence and positive self-image, healthy coping strategies, identifying as a survivor, being connected to supportive others, having a sense of something greater than ourselves, seeking help and resources, finding positive meaning in life, managing feelings, and developing good communications skills.

If you have the resources to hire a life coach, sports coach, nutritionist, therapist, masseuse, stylist, financial planner, and career and relationship gurus, well done, you! But I'll root for a DIY approach. Also, resilience isn't about just taking the hit and getting back up. It's about getting quiet for that inner voice that says, "It's okay, try again. You have this."

It's up to us to listen. We have to respect our soft and hard limits—our emotional and physical boundaries—and practice expressing them. We have to honor our instincts about when to bend or draw the line. We have to know when to push and when to reward and when to say uncle. This is all S&M 101.

Resilience is a mainstay in S&M, and every submissive who has braved a pain threshold by graduating to a tougher whip knows what I'm talking about. Each time a sub cooperates with surrender is a teachable moment. Turns out surrender can be crazy fun, and the kink world is full to the brim with teachable moments!

Redefining your comfort zone in a dungeon equates to going the extra mile in a marathon. Negotiating S&M scenes equates to stipulating a game plan. Creating safewords equates to saying "back off" or "hell no." Expressing fetishes equates to voicing strongly held views. Setting limits equates to creating healthy boundaries. Yes to this, no to that, and most important: this is who I am.

In the movie *Girlfight*, before a pivotal boxing match, Diana (played by Michelle Rodriguez) has a quiet moment with her boxing coach. He asks her, "Inside, you know yourself?" She answers, "Yeah. I do." He says, "Then that's all you need."[1]

So how do we vanilla Janes become our own champion and coach?

Spank This

Practice Gratitude. Every. Single. Day. Whether you journal it or pray it or think it, it's your inroad to happiness. Gratitude is a powerful expression of love from your higher self. Creating the state of joy you'd experience if you got everything you wanted enriches your life and keeps you in the now. It offsets a conditional if-then mindset. As a bonus, being grateful for what you have attracts more good into your life. Use scarcity thinking and negativity as a cue to get into the gratitude mindset—counting your blessings is the best way to rock joy and prosperity. Gratefulness for your circumstances, loved ones, and life force is a form of spirituality heralded by virtually every spiritual leader of Eastern and Western philosophies. Saying thanks is respectful, and it gives the universe a chance to say, "You're welcome."

Jeweled Crown. BDSM limits create physical and emotional boundaries for play, freeing kinksters to get their freak on. Limits are a bad word in vanilla lingo, equated with restrictions and glass ceilings and curbed potential. We have to flip this. Women are often expected to ignore their boundaries—their hard and soft limits—and acquiesce. If we yield to our partner or cave in at the meeting or take our boss's leers, we won't be accused of being uptight or a bitch. This strategy is epically unsustainable and keeps us out of our natural state of femininity. Practicing healthy boundaries helps us feel more centered, take control of our lives, and explore what is true for us. What is true for us creates longevity, the crown jewel of resilience.

Don't "Should" Yourself. Expecting that you, others, and life should conform to your expectations creates misery. With all our softness and flexibility, we women get stuck in the fuckery of expectations. The antidote is practicing realistic optimism. That's taking things as they are while still striving for our ideals. Remember the last time you did something with neutral expectations? Wasn't it easier to enjoy what happened in the present moment? Instead of deciding how things should be, allow whatever arises in the moment. Have intent and know your hard and soft limits, but whatever you are, be it fully. "I want to really show up as me" is less ironhanded than "I have to kick ass." This softer approach leads the way to growth, fun, and flexibility.

Toughen Your Ass. Longtime BDSM players who are into being spanked develop a thick skin, literally and figuratively. There is an art to moving into the pain. While a submissive may beg a domme for a spanking, they still have to practice resilience. He or she has to give themselves to the pain in order to withstand it. This practice prepares the sub for when their limits are inevitably pushed. It also lends itself to life's painful challenges, and embracing challenges strengthens us. The key is to be flexible and avoid seeing stressful events (like hard-landing paddles) as unbearable problems.

Beautiful Mind. The Law of Polarity states that in any situation there must be an opposite—there cannot be a problem without there also being an answer. The answer is built into the problem itself, and you just have to look for it. Problems aren't bad; they're a question in need of an answer. What if you looked at every one of life's challenges like this? Einstein said, "It's not that I'm so smart. It's just that I stay with problems longer."[2] This, my friends, is resilience. If we stay with the problem, we receive the insight, the gift, the life lesson. Don't quit five minutes before your miracle happens. (Thanks in advance, universe!)

Safeword. Lao Tzu, a philosopher of ancient China, wrote the Tao Te Ching. He wisely said, "The master understands that the universe is forever out of control."[3] Think of a Chinese finger trap—the more you pull and struggle, the tighter it becomes. It's a common metaphor for a problem that can be overcome by relaxing and not trying too hard. In other words, know when to get tough and when to say uncle. Or "red," if the handcuffs are too tight.

LMAO. What's the sexiest, smartest thing you can own? (No, not Louboutins.) A sense of humor! Humor helps you keep perspective when life goes MMA on your ass, and finding humor while you're on the mat increases resilience. Have fun! Crack yourself up! Laughing is the best. In the original *Arthur* (my mom's favorite flick), Dudley Moore laughs uproariously and says, "Sometimes I just think funny things!"[4]

Daily Grind. Your devotion to the daily grind—not coffee, but that helps—is resilience. Superwomen endure dark moments of emotional overwhelm and exhaustion to bring their dreams to fruition. That stick-to-itiveness is what nails their success. Take heart in psychologist John Hayes's "ten-year rule": it takes at least a decade of hard work and practice to master anything, from sports to writing books.[5] Embrace repetition. Repetition is the stuff of resilience; it builds muscle memory and new skill circuits in the brain. Revel in that heroic hundredth—or thousandth—effort! It may be the breakthrough to the kick-ass life you've dreamed of.

Mean Vaccine. Beef up your immunity against epic struggles. Think of this as taking homeopathic medicine. Miniscule doses of the thing you want to avoid make you healthier and better able to cope with it when it does strike (just as mini doses of pain builds up a subs tolerance!) Life's knocks prepare us for future difficulties. During tough times, a deeper self emerges, so practice finding meaning in adversity. Mini doses of hardship will keep you in the race.

Lifeline. In BDSM, dominants practice awareness and compassion toward submissives. This makes for a better scene and benefits everyone. Those who look out for others do better than those who save only themselves. The best way to defeat a victim mentality is by taking responsibility for yourself and showing compassion to others. Cultivating a giving attitude in your everyday life will help you build resilience. Volunteering cements this principle—take it from me; you always get more than you give. It's good for the soul, the planet, and your sense of contribution. Give from the heart—anything you do for your fellow man comes back to you.

Imitation Nation. Some people are crazy resilient and survive every adversity with dignity, strength, and forgiveness. Think of whom you admire as role models or heroes. It could be your hometown firefighter, veteran, or elderly neighbor. Maybe it's Dita Von Teese for her mad-sexy burlesque and entrepreneurism—"I'm not the girl who changes into flats because my feet are tired at the end of the night. I go the distance. I go all the way."[6] Maybe it's poet and author Maya Angelou, who symbolized resilience and shook a few tail feathers in her time—"I love to see a young girl go out and grab the world by the lapels. Life's a bitch. You've got to go out and kick ass."[7] Maybe it's Sonia Sotomayor, the first Latina Supreme Court Justice, or Bettie Page, the scandalous 1950s fetish-S&M-bondage pinup icon. Whoever they are, which of their traits do you admire? Are they constantly evolving toward their life vision? Do they seem to accept circumstances that can't be changed? You don't have to reinvent the wheel—keep a mental list of who in your immediate life or in the public eye seems to roll with setbacks. Take a cue from what they do, and if it's not obvious, invite the person to coffee or write a letter and ask.

Post It Up. To acknowledge your accomplishments is to embrace the carrot-over-club approach. By rewarding yourself, you're more likely to welcome the grind. Regular reminders of problems you nailed and the factors that helped you will build you up for the next win. Your efforts are what led to your accomplishments and deserve equal praise, so take the Post-It Note Challenge. Once a week, write down a few efforts—win, lose, or draw—and post them all over to remind you what a badass you are. (Or wiseass, or smartass, or nice ass . . . .)

Natural High. Never underestimate the power of endorphins— a release of these happy hormones creates an elated feeling that can last for hours. Endorphins up your resilience and even relieve depression. You don't have to jog five miles to get a runner's high—sex, yoga, weight training, power play, and nature walks all kick in your happy drug. Belly laughing takes it up to eleven. Other ways to trigger endorphins are positive thinking, eating spicy foods or chocolate, getting emotional, and sunshine. I dare you to plan an orgasmic day that includes reciting a mantra on a sunny hike, crying over a sunset, spanking your sweetie, and eating a spicy dinner followed by chocolate soufflé and your favorite comedy. BAM!

Training. Being a doormat isn't sustainable or sexy. (This goes for you, inner nice girl.) In a dungeon, there's a clear hierarchy in which a dominatrix demands respect from a submissive, and each partner sets the tempo of the relationship early on with clear boundaries. This goes for life in general—you teach people how to treat you, without exception. Your attitude and self-love tell people all they need to know. If you value yourself you'll project self-worth in your interactions and others will see it, feel it, and respond in kind. The people in your life are reflections of your evolution. Luckily, choosing who's right for you is a simple art. Hang around only with nice people! I consider every supportive, kind, genuine person in my life a milestone that reflects my personal growth. It's okay if someone doesn't "get" you, share your values, or speak the language of your soul. Move on.

Sacred Space. BDSM dungeons are highly controlled environments, complete with all the accoutrements that scream, "whip me!" There are specific spaces for acting out sessions with a strong sense of containment—unlike a beautifully messy and unscripted life. Meanwhile, the dungeon environment creates a vibe of existential darkness and mystery. What vibe does your environment create? Being the master of your surroundings can do wonders for your resilience and feelings of control. Maybe you master your environment with Feng Shui. Maybe you create a prayer and meditation space in which to savor the peaceful early morning. Maybe you light candles and play ambient music. Maybe you purge your clutter and donate unwanted objects to charity. Create a sacred space to connect with your higher self and soothe worries.

Practice Mindfulness. Thich Nhat Hanh is a Zen monk and mindfulness teacher. He defines mindfulness as "the energy of being aware and awake to the present . . . the continuous practice of touching life deeply in every moment."[8] He explains that each moment provides an opportunity for mindfulness, and insights from mindfulness can liberate us. Some acts feel more mindful and meditative than others—creating art, being in nature, losing yourself in music, and a no-brainer is eating. I holy-shit-*love* to eat, so it's the easiest time for me to get present while savoring the texture, flavor, and sensation of every mindful bite. Girl's gotta get her grub on.

Studded Umbrella. Let's get real—life is going to put a steel-toe boot up your ass sometimes. There's no way around the certainty of shit storms. No part of your life is immune to things going sideways—not your love life, work life, or family life.

Being resilient is taking what comes and having a damn good umbrella by the door. In a shit storm, you don't invent new behaviors—you fall back on what you've practiced. You're always rehearsing something, whether you know it or not. If you can keep your perspective during a minor hiccup, you can during a crisis. You'll be able to see losing your job as a chance to find your true calling or getting dumped as an invitation for the love of your life to appear. Pick yourself up, and decide on the bigger, better thing that you will now manifest. And keep that umbrella handy for next time.

Buddy Up. Kindergarten pretty much teaches everything you need to know about the resilient power of friendship. Remember at school when the crossing guard had you buddy up? Buddies worked together as a single unit to watch out for and help each other. In kindergarten, there were charming stories about the art of listening, and puppets who role-played making friends by joining in an activity and giving compliments. There was time set aside for rest to keep cranky pants from being mean to each other and time for creativity to express what couldn't be said in words. There were special songs about being kind and talking sticks for taking turns during discussions. There was kissing during recess if you wanted or cooty spray if you didn't. There was praise for being courteous, sports for learning teamwork, and show-and-tell for understanding different points of view. Really . . . is there anything more than this?

ON COURAGE

It isn't ever delicate to live. *—Kay Ryan*

Humans are so adaptable. Once broken, we become super humanly strong—forged from steel bones. Once violated, we vacate our bodies and emotional cores, forgoing softness to survive. But the real journey is to move beyond surviving to thriving. To balance fear with self-trust.

Unlearning the fear of exposing my heart has been a lifelong gig. By the time I was twenty, I rocked hella bravado. I said "later" to emotional risks and hid my sensitivity. I stomped around in combat boots and never once checked whether it was me or my fear talking. I sabotaged relationships and hid my girliness to keep from getting hurt. It pained me that people missed seeing my huggable, goofy self, but closeness scared me more.

I began to champion underdogs in my writing, volunteering as a crisis counselor, and serving the homeless. I fell in love with humanity and people's imperfections but refused to accept my own. The pain of hiding from the world held a message: meeting fear head-on was way less scary than living with its underlying helplessness.

My bravado had to evolve. Instead of steeling myself for every potential kick in the teeth, instead of living the daily me-versus-everything, instead of hiding, I asked myself what good could happen—you know, if I actually showed up to my own life.

I taped a quote by Goethe to my bathroom mirror: "Just trust yourself, then you will know how to live." My mantra became, "I've *got* this!" (even as my teeth were chattering). Getting naked as an author upped the ante because the writing had to be entirely, authentically me. The upside was that the focus shifted from me to my message.

The truth is, you teach what you need to learn. You give away what you want. There are lots of paths that help you evolve. I was inspired to serve those in need more by losing my mother than by selflessness, but it resulted in opening my heart. Childhood abuse was dehumanizing, but it created a humanitarian. Overcoming is the mark of a survivor and proves the beauty of the human spirit.

Setting an intention to live from the heart draws people who are good for you. The heart wants to be known. The sheer terror and beauty of that takes my breath away. If you let the heart lead, your wall of fear will crack just enough to manifest someone who you can share your true, swaggering self with. You can say too much and be too much, and this person will stick around. In spite of everything, because of everything, you brought this into being. You have the little heart that could.

Living a heart-based life is fucking delicious and utterly feminine. It's worth fighting for. It helps if what you want outweighs what you fear. It helps if you are wildly curious and maybe even a little desperate. My need to reclaim my life overcame my fear of the dark, deviant S&M world. I moved *toward* the fear, not away from it, which is a hallmark of BDSM.

Kinksters flip the fear script. They relax when pain is coming at them and move into it, which is counterintuitive but crushes fear. They arch into the biting tail of a bullwhip instead of running, firing up their endorphins and their erotic zones. They opt for the hard paddle and the scary Mistress. Sometimes it's about taking a deep breath and baring your ass.

I wouldn't have these takeaways if I hadn't dommed up. I wouldn't have learned about the opulence of pain, the many shades of bravery, and the significance of granting and receiving power. I definitely wouldn't have rocked thigh-high stiletto boots (bonus points!).

UNCHAINED COURAGE

Those who do not move, do not notice their chains.
—*Rosa Luxemburg*

Ever read the story of the mouse that became mighty? Scientists genetically modified its sense of smell to switch off its fear of cats. This newly brave mighty mouse snuggled up to a cat and gave it a smooch.[1]

The win is the "unlearning" of the mouse experiment. If you tunnel under the indoctrinated ideas of your supposed self, you might find a dragon slayer, an aerialist, or a Nobel Prize winner. The possibilities are endless. The question is, what would you do and be if you weren't scared?

Most of us hate feeling scared, unless we're in a popcorn-scented theater or on a hells-yeah rollercoaster. Helpless *real life* fear is the worst. But unlike the engineered mighty mouse, we need to be in touch with our fear—it's our primordial tipoff to danger. It's what we do with fear that counts.

That's why the smartest advice is taking action in spite of fear, not pressuring yourself to conquer fear. Having our cage rattled proves we're living and growing. Better to think in terms of an inner warrior who thrives on battle.

If your only job is to meet fear with action, it's easier to battle train your warrior. Sometimes warrior training is about getting present for the smell of honeysuckle, sometimes it's learning mixed martial arts, and sometimes it's letting go. The end goal is to trust yourself.

I feared S&M for the same reason most people do: because I didn't understand it. I was scared shitless to walk into a dungeon but *knew* there was something there for me. So much of the experience was about fear at first: What if I hurt someone? What if I couldn't handle the intensity? What if I lost my childlike wonder? What if I liked it too much? I had to trust that I could handle whatever happened.

Fear wasn't the only thing I spanked. Consenting submissives begged for all-out torture or humiliation, and guess who was the enforcer? It could be emotionally conflicting to be the punisher and the protector, wholly responsible for a sub's well-being during a scene. Sometimes I got lost in the flow and had to remind myself to monitor their body language and emotional signals. Other times the intensity (or the hilarity of role-play) was nearly too much.

I faced BDSM taboos because I knew there was a payoff. (Besides a foot fetishist painting my toenails Chanel red with his teeth.) There's always a payoff in fear. The thing about bravery is, no matter the life lesson, the act of facing fear head-on is its own reward.

I did it are the three most powerful words, after *I love you*.

Like any good journey, my dominatrix detour had a beginning, a middle, and an end. I took power play to the master level, pun intended. The art of domination helped liberate me, and the lessons of the dungeon were instilled in me. They influence my vanilla life every day.

Don't let fear keep you from your full potential. You are a fierce heroine! Act on faith if you don't believe it yet. Play-act your heroine into being in small ways, like trusting that you're okay in this one moment. Build risks into your life practice and don't lose out on the payoffs of fear.

How else can we vanilla Janes trust ourselves and nurture our bravery?

Spank This

Get Curious. Getting curious about what scares the bejesus out of you is an overlooked strategy. It works in the dungeon and it works in everyday life. When we're curious, we genuinely want to see things in a new way, which gets us present. This tends to defuse fear. Curiosity sparks the jones to *find out*, which makes the world inviting instead of scary. It creates openness to unfamiliar experiences and the unknown. As a bonus, curiosity is a sign of intelligence, it leads to life meaning and purpose, and it improves relationships. Oh, and it's crazy sexy.

Me First. Trusting that you'll keep yourself safe starts with being safe. That might mean cutting out self-deprecation and perfectionism. It might mean hanging around with nicer people, accepting compliments, and scheduling joy. It will definitely mean putting yourself first. It's whatever sends the message that you'll do the most loving thing for yourself in every situation. An example is that I put my well-being first in the dungeon. If a sub had a bad vibe, was lewd or misogynistic—especially if he tried to shame me for my limits—I would walk. This only happened twice and both times the subs apologized (one even said he felt terrible since his sister was a feminist!). This has helped me to stand up for myself in everyday situations. A "me first" attitude should always be based in love. To love yourself through your fears, write down the scariest thing you want to do and the fear that's keeping you from doing it. "I want X, but I'm afraid of Y." Keep taking steps toward it, while giving yourself pep talks and congrats along the way. Nail this practice, and become a bravehearted, joyful Jane.

Lean In. Embracing fear can set you free. You know the advice about turning your steering wheel into the direction of a skid? Fear is like that. It seems bassackwards, but leaning in to fear is the way to control its momentum. Fear can spiral you out of control, and anyone's first impulse would be to try to run in the other direction—but trust me, you have to lean into that shit. That takes a lot of trust in yourself and the process, and those are muscles that can be developed if you work at them. In BDSM, the more you lean into your fear the more it liberates you. The more you soften, the deeper you can delve into your bliss. Giving up control, even when scary, allows a more evolved "control."

Role-Play. Role-playing isn't just about getting kinky with *Cosmo* BDSM sex tips; it's an all-around, everyday power practice for vanillas out of the bedroom (and dungeon) too. Have someone safe assume the role of a loved one or colleague that you're afraid to confront. Take on the posture and tone you'd be using if you actually confronted this person, and have him or her interact with you while you think on your feet. There is no therapuetic limit to the role-playing you can get into in a dungeon! Teachers, bullies, crappy bosses, and cruel fathers are all game. Stay in character! Let it out! When you've nailed the role-play, hug it out and discuss ways that you could have been more effective. Practice asking your role-play buddy for a raise or asking strangers for what you want to make the real deal easier. If you really want to get adventurous with role-play, show up at a costume party or fetish ball disguised as your alter ego and get all up in there.

Scaredy Is as Scaredy Does. Psychological boundaries can keep you safe. Who better to take boundary advice from than an admitted scaredy cat? You, too, can replace your armored fifty-foot walls with a filigreed dressing screen. Fewer defenses are where it's at. Giving or receiving help connects you to community, while "back the fuck off" is the ultimate defense mantra. Susanna Bair, a leader of heart-centered living, knows what's up about defensive boundaries. She says, "This is a model of isolation, and it's not holistic, healthy, or necessary. The alternative is intentional vulnerability, which gains us closeness and authenticity."[2] In kink, the ultimate tool to create boundaries and vulnerability is a safeword. This concept can carry over into your vanilla life: diligently using a mental safeword for your personal well-being (when your boundaries are threatened) allows you to let your guard down. If we practice intentional vulnerability, we get to be brave and real? Done! Badasses need hugs too.

Action Doll. A half hour of physical activity will put the burn on fear. Physical exertion burns off anxiety—whether it's sprinting, heavy lifting, a dungeon scene, or an impromptu dance party. Just pick up the weights (or the paddle) or crank up your jam and burn that shit out. Working out increases your confidence and courage and is a great way to manage your emotions to keep rolling.

Take the Test. I believe that trusting in something greater than yourself fuels bravery, but not trusting in *yourself* fuels fear. Test it out: Fear of leaving a shitty relationship equals not trusting that you can handle being alone. Fear of talking to your crush equals not trusting that you can handle the pain of rejection. Fear of the unknown equals not trusting that you can handle the future. Fear of the dark equals not trusting that you can handle the boogie monster. Which boogie monsters hold you back?

Make a Mantra. You can program the subconscious with affirmations—those seemingly dorky Pollyanna sayings. You don't even have to believe affirmations for them to work. Just keep repeating them. The mind reacts to what it's fed, whether it's true or false. You can either let scary stuff have its way with you or listen to your higher self. Create a personal mantra that resonates. Make sure it's positive and in the present tense, like "I am the heroine of my own life" or "I knock out problems in my sleep!"

Make Nice with the Big Other. Trusting the universe is kind of a big deal. Whatever it takes, you owe it to yourself to find some good in the world. Seeing the world as scary and punishing will fuel fears and negativity. Look for signs that the world is loving and forgiving and has your back. The proof is there. Repeat this mantra in spite of your doubt: "The universe is abundant." Abundance starts in your heart. *You* are the change. Give away what you most want to get. Performing acts of kindness will help change your perception about how cruel or kind the world is. Pay for the person behind you in line, smile at a stranger, volunteer, give a Kind bar wrapped in a dollar and a Snoopy ribbon to someone in need—these are my favorites. Random acts of kindness are limitless, so pay it forward!

Whip Smart. Sometimes fear is like an ass-whipping—intense and coming at you with full force. If you could withstand the fear of a striking bullwhip, you could handle anything, right? To hone your self-trust for everyday fears, conquer some epic ones. Challenge yourself to something that scares the bejesus out of you such as zip-lining, public speaking, dungeon domination, or clown wrangling. Then the little things will be a breeze.

Right Here, Right Now. Money, right? The other 99 percent of you know what I'm talking about. When I decided to go all-in as a writer, I began plundering my savings to fund my passion. I admitted my all-in strategy to a financial planner who said, "You're making the smartest investment you can make. You're investing in yourself!" Still, financial insecurity led to panic, which cemented one of the greatest life lessons: *get present*. Getting present diminishes threats and grounds you in the here and now. I practiced mindfulness by creating a state of *openness* to abundance, *awareness* to the music or sunlight surrounding me, and *focus* on my life vision. Mindfulness one, fear zero. Free yourself by asking this simple question: "Am I okay right now? In this moment?" Chances are, the answer will be yes.

Go Watergate on Fear's Ass. Write down your secret fears and then get rid of them. Do a free-form writing exercise and get real about what you're afraid of. All of it. Now, shred it! This is symbolic, sure—like doing a role-play scene in a dungeon to rid yourself of a phobia—but it's a way to release your biggest fears from your body, get them onto the paper, and then to turn them into harmless shreds. Nixon was onto something.

Happy Face. Showing kindness to even one other human makes the world better. The quickest kindness anyone can extend is a smile. Just grin at someone for no damn reason. If you're shy (like me) or worried about giving a stranger an "in" (oh, the drama), trust yourself to keep a safe social distance. The perks of smiling are that you get to pay it forward, you get to practice self-trust, and you get to feel good. Smiling is an on switch for your brain and actually makes you happier. Win-win-win!

Go Deep. Losing yourself in something that taps into your passion (or joys you up) is a sure-fire cure for fear. For me, writing immersion is the bliss of timeless, euphoric space. Nothing else feels as joyful, even on days when every word is hard won. What's your bliss? Use whatever resonates for you, even if it's the delicious trance-like state of subspace (or topspace).

Verbal Math. What if you could zap fear and practice kindness at the same time? You can by listening. Listening is an act of reverence. It requires getting present and taking the focus off yourself. You may be the only outlet for what's in someone's heart and mind. That's a privilege. Listening is a way to honor your fellow human, be it a neighbor or a homeless person. Some people aren't afforded a voice in life—you can change this. I know I'm on my fucking soapbox here, but I will always champion those in need. Crisis counseling on a suicide hotline taught me skills I try to use in everyday life: Be an advocate, not an authority. Don't trivialize someone's needs and feelings—I wouldn't mock a sub's secret fantasies any more than I would mock someone in crisis. Don't check out until it's your turn. Hear someone's story, and inquire when there's space. Paraphrase what you hear and empathize. Active listening equals respect.

Unlearn Fight or Flight. Back in the (prehistoric) day, our ancestors lived in a world in which danger was ever present. Wild animals would prey on you, rival clans were out to get you, and Neanderthal dudes would club you over the head as soon as you dropped your guard. It was crucial to have an urgent danger-response system. This created what amounts to a glitch in the human brain that causes us to interpret scary emotions as life threatening. Your work is to practice nonreaction in the face of *incorrectly perceived* danger, not actual danger (like a run-away truck). The goal is to be nonreactive, centered, and calm. Moderating your knee-jerk responses allows you to access inner wisdom, and it's not the same as denying your instincts. If you feel wary about a person or tense about a situation, listen. Denying, rationalizing, and minimizing your raised hackles will get you in trouble. Consider whether it's a saber-toothed tiger or a housefly you're worried about.

Love Bound. Sometimes courage means setting boundaries and standing up for yourself even if it pisses someone off. It's about choosing what's best for your well-being. It's honoring your limits; noticing what makes you feel violated, hurt, or scared; cherishing what makes you feel safe; and expressing what's acceptable to you. Showing up for yourself in these ways is the kinder, gentler psychological defense. It's also a staple of BDSM. Ask yourself this powerful question in every situation: What's the most loving choice in this moment? You'll begin showing more compassion to yourself and others.

Truth or Dare. Face your fears for one day by only doing things that resonate as true to who you are. Prompt yourself with questions. What do I value? What's fun for me? What do I want to create? Where's my mojo? Don't overthink it, just express it. For one day, dare to wear that fave outfit you're afraid will draw stares, go to a play party if that's your leaning, read your groovy poem at a poetry slam, just *show up* in your own unique way. Seriously. Right now, open your calendar and schedule your bravery.

Soft and Brave. Brené Brown is an author and leading researcher in the study of vulnerability, courage, worthiness, and shame. She makes a strong case for vulnerability in her TED Talk. The gist of her talk is that human connection is the basis for everything—it's why we're here. The thing that unravels it is shame, which is the fear of disconnection. You hide something because if it's seen or known, it will make you unworthy of connection. Brown found that people who had a sense of worthiness were connected as a result of their authenticity. They fully embraced vulnerability and believed that what made them vulnerable also made them beautiful.[3] This was a fairly radical concept for me to absorb, and I remind myself all the time that it's true. Brown found that people try to selectively numb vulnerability, which also numbs joy, gratitude, and happiness, leaving us miserable. Her secret to happiness is to let yourself be seen, love with your whole heart, practice gratitude and joy, and believe that you're enough. That's crazy brave.

Giddy Up. Did I mention the power of laughter? The essentialness of play? Reveling in giddiness purges fear and self-consciousness. Irish playwright Seán O'Casey drives the point home: "Laughter is wine for the soul—laughter soft, or loud and deep, tinged through with seriousness—the hilarious declaration made by [wo]man that life is worth living."[4] So it is.

WHERE KINK MEETS VANILLA

God may be in the details, but the goddess
is in the questions. Once we begin to ask them,
there's no turning back. —*Gloria Steinem*

Every day we make decisions about how we show up, claim our worth, love our bodies, roll with challenges, and trust ourselves. In choosing our truths we become more—more divine, more empowered, more of who we are meant to be.

Our daily practice can actualize our potential, one spank at a time. We can embrace our identity with the authenticity spanks. We can celebrate our worth with the confidence spanks. We can honor our bods with the body image spanks. We can roll past obstacles with the resilience spanks. We can rock bravery with the courage spanks. Life spanks empower us to live our truth.

It's no surprise to you by now that this way of being is practiced in BDSM. With the right mindset and a little flip in context, many philosophies found in the world of kink are pretty useful in a vanilla world, wouldn't you say? BDSM can help you connect with your body, heart, and mind in a meaningful way.

Integrating these practices into our vanilla lives deepens our purpose. It helps us rethink our beauty and strength. And it honors the quiet, heart-based part of us that doesn't need outside validation—the "I am" that makes each of us Janes wholly unique. And already flawless.

$\mathcal{L}$ACE UP, GODDESS JANES

How 'bout remembering your divinity.
—Alanis Morissette, "Thank You"

I'm honored to support you on your heroine's journey. I have shared wisdom that I have found to be useful, healing, and even life changing. I've offered creative, spiritual, and revolutionary life teachers as collective inspiration. It's all about the mojo.

I hope I've inspired you to wear your body with pride, bend strong with resilience, and leap into your fear. To get heart-naked and butt-naked. I hope you'll live with grace and intention, gently lean into your heart, and rock your truth. And always, always, rise to your own potential.

Gandhi said, "My life is my message."[1] Will you sign your message with *absofuckinglutely*? Will you celebrate yourself? Will you be kind and serve others with your gifts? Will you open your heart and be brave? *Hell yes!* You will choose you.

Every moment is a brand-new chance to shine. Each second is the right one to step into you. Right now, you have permission to rise above. You can create a new intention and start fresh. We all get do-overs; it's part of the human gig. The fact that life gives us do-overs is proof of its kindness.

Only one thing is required—not a sojourn to India or a near-death experience or a diamond ring. That one thing is *choosing*. Too simple, you say? Repeat after me: "I, goddess, choose to shine from this moment on."

Choosing begins your life transformation. Spiritual mindfulness teacher Eckhart Tolle says, "Realize deeply that the present moment is all you have. Make the NOW the primary focus of your life."[2] Your power is in the present, and being in the moment is a VIP pass to your best self.

Right now, decide to reinvent yourself, do what you love, or discover your meaning. Vote yes for something, and commit to it. Deciding not to choose is surrendering power and saying that you're not worth it. Oh *hell* no. You are a sacred feminine badass, a goddess, an extraordinary Jane!

Your choice sets everything in motion. Don't let the bigness overwhelm you—start small. Choose you in this moment. Choose yourself like your life depends on it.

As you walk your own path, be willing to fall. Be willing to purge your closet, your frenemies, your excuses, and your apathy. Be willing to be crazy scared, because the good stuff waits on the other side of that.

You are evolution in action. You wouldn't have read this far if that were not true. Your change is from the inside out. It starts from the deep you that was always there. Do you feel it? It's divine, limitless, and the keeper of the groove.

Let's become our own heroines. Let's rise above our limits to rock our lives. Let's fuck up and make messes, laugh and love. Let's be true to ourselves even when it ain't pretty. Let's trust ourselves, bring the sexy, and swagger into the wild unknown. We're in this together, arms linked and hips swaying.

It's go time. Just take a stiletto step. Shout what you want as if anything were possible, and then give thanks and say, "This or something better now manifests for me."

Well done, you.

$\mathcal{P}$ARTING SPANK

Sometimes evolving means moving on, once we've gotten the insights we need. I had entered into the kink scene to discover new things about myself, see the world through a different lens, and immerse myself in all things "power." Midway through a BDSM scene, I realized my perception of power had evolved from absolute badassery to compassionate strength, and it turned out to be my last time in a dungeon.

That night I'd met a Midwestern guy named Danny at a fetish club's bondage demo. He was eager and curious, and after the demo he confided that he desperately wanted to give up control. "And if I don't get spanked soon I'll lose my mind," he joked.

I asked him how he wanted to play, and he said he wanted to try light pain and bondage. He didn't want to be on display, tortured, or humiliated. "I definitely don't want some man hater who's into dishing out pain."

I assured him that I didn't have a score to settle with our patriarchal culture and that my humanity was intact. I told him a lot of kinksters use S&M as a path to self-actualization. When I told him I was into nonsexual dominance, he asked why.

I replied, "You'll find that power play has lots of layers and intimacy, without sex. It's like how running is less about putting one foot in front of the other than about how it frees you."

"I get that," he said. "What's missing for me runs deeper than sex."

"Bingo."

"Is that my safeword?"

I laughed. "No, but it can be."

By this point the after-demo play party was starting, and we agreed to a session. I grabbed my bag to change into my fetish gear; leather corset with a laced back, black pencil skirt, and stilettos. A swipe of eyeliner and cherry lip-gloss and I was good to go.

Other females prowled through the dungeon, poured into latex dresses, satin corsets, and towering boots. Boss ass bitches, one and all. Some guys wore jeans and button-down shirts, others looked to be auditioning for *Leatherman Monthly*. Dark, ethereal music flooded the room. Overhead was a suspension device, archaic-looking with metal hooks. Danny winced up at it.

"You're safe," I said. "If you want to be."

The beauty of dungeon parties is that they're monitored. There're seasoned kinksters playing openly while newbies can mingle and explore, which makes them less nervous. I told the dungeon monitor with a Bettie Page haircut that I had a shy newbie. She appraised Danny then led us down a dark hallway, past a room with a spanking bench, cage, and whipping post—"for worship and torture," she explained to Danny.

Guttural moans came from farther down the hall. As my eyes adjusted to the dark I could see a woman being whipped with a cat-o'-nine-tails. She wore only a G-string; long blond hair spilled over her shoulders.

The dominant was athletic and shirtless, dressed in 501s over polished square-toe boots. He had a kind of presence, a physical alertness. He sent the whip into her while saying quietly, "Beautiful...surrender...*push*." His soft assurances against the whip's clap were more potent than brute force. The sub arched her back and met the whip with gulping breaths.

I glanced at Danny's mesmerized expression, likely the same one I wore when I first began my BDSM exploration.

We were led to a dim-lit room with a red sofa, gilded mirror, X-cross, and spanking bench. The scent of leather and sweat hung in the air. "Enjoy," the monitor said, handing me a one-hour *Private Playtime* sign. I hung the sign on the door and clicked it softly behind me.

I prided myself on connecting with subs in a way that they never had to use a safeword. Still, I told Danny to use *yellow* if he wanted me to slow down, and *red* if he wanted me to stop.

"And *bingo* if I want more?"

I chuckled. "You are a corn-fed wonder. Ready?"

He gave a bobble headed nod.

I slipped into my role and took out a lightweight wooden paddle, a black leather paddle, a purple suede flogger, and a short crop. "Any preference?"

"All of them!"

"Good answer," I said. "Now kneel."

He dropped to his knees and gazed up at me. After a weighted silence I said, "You have one minute to undress and face the X-cross." I then left the room. I intuited that he needed to be alone as he stripped himself physically and bared himself emotionally.

When I opened the door Danny stood facing the X-cross. I tucked his wrists and ankles into the bondage cuffs and gave his bare ass a pat to bring the blood to the surface. The skin-to-skin contact would help to connect and prepare him.

He wiggled and I lightly grabbed his hair. "You want to please me?"

"More than anything," he said.

"Then be still and surrender."

"*Yes*, goddess."

"Now count out your swats."

Smack! The first swat made him flinch.

"*One*," he called out.

When we got to ten, I took up the flogger and stroked it along his back. "Ass out!" I ordered, and lightly landed the tails against him a few times, to get him used to it. I told him to relax into the sensation until his body began to soften, absorbing the intensifying blows as he accepted the pain.

"You're doing beautifully," I said. I loved how he gave himself to our exchange. He was trusting and present in a way which helped center me, too.

Every lesson that I'd ever learned about power—from horses to subs, from boundaries to surrender—came down to compassionate strength. I felt it deeply in this moment. Being in my power took mindfulness, which brought me full circle. Suddenly I thought, so I get to be a badass warrior and be *nice?* That works!

I savored the moment and kept an eye on Danny's breathing and body language. After a bit I walked over and rested my hand on his chest, over his heart. "All good?"

Slowly he nodded his head. "Bingo."

And the next half hour was bliss. From flogger to paddle, caress to strike, you become one with it all. My flogging took on the rhythm of the music, landing in time with the slow and heavy drumbeats. Danny had gone from shallow, quick breaths to the core breathing that was common with trance-like subspace.

When I finally slowed to the last whip and gave him his last swat, I removed his restraints and he smiled goofily. "Thank you," he mumbled, disoriented.

I helped him to the couch and kissed the top of his head as we slumped shoulder to shoulder. Danny was an ideal play partner for me—unassuming, giving, grateful, and all about exploring his true self. Maybe he'd find that kink was his orientation, and want a lasting Domme/sub relationship. I had earned and owned the title of domme. But I knew, sitting next to Danny in all his newbie glory, that if kink was his thing, he deserved an innate kinkster.

Gently I asked, "How you feeling, wonder boy?"

He paused. "Kind of spacey...but good. It felt more hypnotic than painful, after a while."

"Aw, your first subspace!" I joked.

"Really?"

"Felt a little like flying?" I asked.

He nodded. "The whole thing was...sexy as fuck."

I laughed. "Therein lies the difference between sensual and sexual. What was your favorite thing?"

He thought about it. "I felt alive, man. I got to be myself and tap into something rad."

I nodded, thinking how those were the things I loved best about it, too. Except for getting to be the boss ass bitch, of course. I got to show up in a way that felt truthful, beautiful, resilient, and courageous. Moving on felt sweet, right, and a little sad. I gave thanks for all of it, and without closing the book, I turned the page.

$\mathcal{W}$ISDOM SPANKS

As your final inspiration I offer wise speeches from five women who are by turns elegant, bawdy, quirky, whip-smart, and poetic. Like all of us.

Wisdom Spank: On Authenticity

"Whatever you choose, however many roads you travel, I hope that you choose not to be a lady. I hope you will find some way to break the rules and make a little trouble out there. And I also hope that you will choose to make some of that trouble on behalf of women."[1]

—**Nora Ephron**, writer and director

Wisdom Spank: On Confidence

"I want to throw my hands in the air, after reading a mean Twitter comment, and say, 'All right! You got it. You figured me out. I'm not pretty. I'm not thin. I do not deserve to use my voice. I'll start wearing a burqa and start waiting tables at a pancake house. All my self-worth is based on what you can see.' But then I think, *Fuck that*. I am a woman with thoughts and questions and shit to say. I say if I'm beautiful. I say if I'm strong. You will not determine my story—I will. I stand here and I am amazing, for you. Not because of you. I am not who I sleep with. I am not my weight. I am not my mother. I am myself. And I am all of you, and I thank you."[2]

—**Amy Schumer**, stand-up comedian and writer

Wisdom Spank: On Body Image

"Your problem is how you are going to spend this one odd and precious life you have been issued. Whether you're going to spend it trying to look good and creating the illusion that you have power over people and circumstances, or whether you are going to taste it, enjoy it and find out the truth about who you are. There are so many great things to do right now. Write. Sing. Rest. Eat cherries . . . and—oh my God—I nearly forgot the most important thing: refuse to wear uncomfortable pants, even if they make you look really thin. Promise me you'll never wear pants that bind or tug or hurt, pants that have an opinion about how much you've just eaten. The pants may be lying!"[3]

—**Anne Lamott**, author and activist

Wisdom Spank: On Resilience

"Feel your strength and your vulnerability. Acknowledge your goodness, and don't be afraid of it. Look at your darkness—and work to understand it, so you'll have the power to choose who you'll be in the world. Women: look at your toughness and your softness. You can and should make room for both in your life. The world needs both. . . . Live and write your own story and then be brave enough to communicate it authentically. Trust me, someone else will be inspired by it and learn from it."[4]

—**Maria Shriver**, author and journalist

Wisdom Spank: On Courage

"Of all your attributes—your youth, your beauty, your wit, your kindnesses, your money—courage is indeed your greatest achievement. It is the greatest of all your virtues, for without courage you cannot practice any other virtue with consistency.

What you have first is your courage. You may lean against it, it will hold you up, you have that. And the joy of achievement, the ecstasy of achievement. It enlightens and lightens at the same time. You are phenomenal. I believe that women are phenomenal. I know us to be."

—**Maya Angelou**, author and activist

$\mathcal{A}$CKNOWLEDGMENTS

Big ups from the heart! To my girlfriends who love me and think *I'm all that*—back atcha. To my beloveds who light up my world, including RS for being my steadfast champion and lovelight. To anyone who has shown me kindness or saw my potential even when I didn't. To the power of do-overs, determination, and divinity. To all the wounded for your courage, and every woman who paved the way. To my agent Angela Rinaldi, and my editor Anna Noak, for both being so charmed by this book as to become its champions. To Anna and

Lindsay at Beyond Words, for helping this little book become so much mightier. To Ava and Badu, for curling up beside me as I write. To my mother, always my mother, for doing her best with what she had been given. To all of my sisters, known and unknown, for standing in grace. And to all my vanilla and not-so-vanilla readers, for keeping the groove!

*N*OTES

SETTING THE SCENE

1. Stephanie Pappas, "Bondage Benefits: BDSM Practitioners Healthier Than 'Vanilla' People," *LiveScience*, May 29, 2013, http://www.live science.com/34832-bdsm-healthy-psychology.html.
2. Rainer Maria Rilke, *Book of Hours: Love Poems to God*, 100th Anniversary Edition, trans. Anita Barrows and Joanna Macy (New York: Riverhead Books, 2005), 119.

On Authenticity

1. Lisa McCourt, "Top 10 Ways to Be Comfortable in Your Own Skin," *Sources of Insight*, January 11, 2012, http://sourcesofinsight.com/top-10-ways-to-be-comfortable-in-your-own-skin.

2. Wendy Weikal-Beauchat, *Courage for the Journey: Wisdom for the Broken Road* (Bloomington, IN: Author House, 2013), 45.

3. Robin Chaddock, *How to Get a Smart Mouth: The Power Of Using Your Words Wisely* (Eugene, OR: Harvest House Publishers, 2008), 171.

4. "Uncool," *Almost Famous*, directed by Cameron Crowe (Los Angeles, CA: DreamWorks Home Entertainment, 2001), DVD.

5. Ashton Applewhite, Tripp Evans, and Andrew Frothingham, *And I Quote: The Definitive Collection of Quotes, Sayings, and Jokes for the Contemporary Speechmaker*, rev. ed. (New York: Thomas Dunne Books, 2003), 331.

6. Marianne Williamson, *A Return to Love: Reflections on the Principles of A Course in Miracles* (New York: HarperCollins, 1992), 190–91.

On Confidence

1. Williamson, *A Return to Love*, 190–91.

2. Amy Cuddy, "Your Body Language Shapes Who You Are," TED Global Talk video, 21:02, filmed June 2012, posted October 2012, http://www.ted.com/talks/amy_cuddy_your_body_language_shapes_who_you_are.

3. Joseph Demakis, *The Ultimate Book of Quotations* (Raleigh, NC: Lulu Press, 2012), 67.

4. Erika Andersen, "If You Want to Succeed in Business, Read More Novels," *Forbes*, May 2012, http://www.forbes.com/sites/erikaandersen/2012/05/31/if-you-want-to-succeed-in-business-read-more-novels/.

5. Johnny Carson, *The Tonight Show Starring Johnny Carson*, season 29, episode 170, directed by Bobby Quinn, aired September, 11, 1991, (New York: NBC Studios), television.

6. Olivia Fox Cabane, *The Charisma Myth: How Anyone Can Master the Art and Science of Personal Magnetism* (New York: Portfolio/Penguin, 2012).

7. Byron Katie, *Loving What Is: Four Questions That Can Change Your Life* (New York: Three Rivers Press, 2003), 82–94.

8. "Stuart Smalley's Famous Quote," YouTube video, 0:07, *Saturday Night Live*, season 16, episode 298, aired February 9, 1991, directed by Dave Wilson, posted by sloneramone, September 29, 2010, https://www .youtube.com/watch?v=-DIETlxquzY.

On Body Image

1. Cameron Russell, "Looks Aren't Everything. Believe Me, I'm a Model," TEDxMidAtlantic, 9:37, filmed October 2012, posted January 2013, http://www.ted.com/talks/cameron_russell_looks_aren_t_everything _believe_me_i_m_a_model.

2. Yvette Malamud Ozer, *A Student Guide to Health: Understanding the Facts, Trends, and Challenges*, (Santa Barbara, CA: Greenwood Publishing Group, 2012), 1:142.

3. Anne Lamott, "Four Secrets That Can Lead to Self-Acceptance," *Oprah*, October 23, 2013, http://www.oprah.com/spirit/The-Path-to-Self -Acceptance-Anne-Lamott.

4. Eleanor Roosevelt, *The Reader's Digest* 37, no. 221 (1940): 84.

5. Geneen Roth, *Women, Food and God: An Unexpected Path to Almost Everything* (New York: Scribner, 2009), 174–75.

6. Anne Lamott, *Bird by Bird: Some Instructions on Writing and Life* (New York: Anchor, 1994), 28.

7. The Vedanta Society of Western Washington explains, "The most fundamental teaching in Vedanta (Hinduism) is that all that exists is divine. Thus every human being is innately divine. And the ultimate goal of life is to manifest this inherent divinity." See http://www.vedanta-seattle.org/what-is-vedanta.

ON RESILIENCE

1. "Hector and Diana," *Girlfight*, directed by Karyn Kusama, (2000; Culver City. Screen Gems/Columbia TriStar, 2001), DVD.

2. Albert Einstein, quoted in Paulo Coelho, "10 Lessons from Einstein," *Paulo Coelho's Blog* (blog), March 16, 2012, http://paulocoelhoblog.com/2012/03/16/10-lessons-from-einstein.

3. Lao Tzu, Tao Te Ching, quoted in Ken Goffman and Dan Joy, *Counterculture through the Ages: From Abraham to Acid House* (New York: Random House, 2007), 67.

4. "Arthur and Gloria sit in his Rolls Royce," *Arthur*, directed by Steve Gordon (Los Angeles: Orion Pictures, 1981. Warner Home Video, 1997), DVD.

5. S. B. Kaufman and J. C. Kaufman, "Ten Years to Expertise, Many More to Greatness: An Investigation of Modern Writers," *Journal of Creative Behavior* 41, no. 2 (2007): 114–124, http://scottbarrykaufman.com/wp-content/uploads/2011/06/Kaufman-Kaufman-2007.pdf.

6. Dita Von Teese, BrainyQuote.com, 2015, http://www.brainyquote.com/quotes/quotes/d/ditavontee513117.html, accessed April 15, 2015.

7. Maya Angelou, BrainyQuote.com, 2015. http://www.brainyquote.com/quotes/quotes/m/mayaangelo578847.html, accessed April 15, 2015.

8. Thich Nhat Hanh, *Happiness: Essential Mindfulness Practices* (Berkley: Paralax Press, 2009), ix.

On Courage

1. Universities of Tokyo and Osaka, "Innate versus Learned Odour Processing in the Mouse Olfactory Bulb," *Nature* 450 (2007): 503–08.
2. Susanna Bair, "Are You Strong Enough to Be Vulnerable?" *The Huffington Post*, April 4, 2013, http://www.huffingtonpost.com/susanna-bair /vulnerability_b_2999783.html.
3. Brené Brown, "The Power of Vulnerability," TEDxHuston, 20:19, filmed June 2010, posted December 2010, http://www.ted.com/talks /brene_brown_on_vulnerability.
4. Seán O'Casey, *The Green Crow* (New York: George Braziller, 1956), 226.

Lace Up, Goddess Janes

1. Mahatma Gandhi, BrainyQuote.com, 2015, http://www.brainyquote .com/quote/quotes/m/mahatmagan105686.html, accessed April 15, 2015.
2. Eckhart Tolle, *The Power of Now: A Guide to Spiritual Enlightenment* (Novato: New World Library, 1999), 30.

Wisdom Spanks

1. Nora Ephron, "Nora Ephron '62 Addressed the Graduates in 1996" (commencement speech, Wellesley College, Wellesley, MA, June 3, 1996), Wellesley College Website, http://www.wellesley.edu/events /commencement/archives/1996commencement.
2. Amy Schumer, (acceptance speech, Gloria Awards and Gala, hosted by the Ms. Foundation for Women, May 1, 2014), quoted in Jennifer Vineyard, "Read Amy Schumer's Powerful Speech about Confidence,"

Vulture, http://www.vulture.com/2014/05/read-amy-schumers-ms-gala -speech.html.

3. Anne Lamott (commencement speech, University of California at Berkeley, Berkeley, California, May 15, 2003), http://www.graduation wisdom.com/speeches/0043-lamott.htm.

4. Maria Shriver (commencement speech, University of Southern California, Annenberg School, Los Angeles, California, 2012), http:// mariashriver.com/blog/2012/05/power-of-the-pause-maria-shriver -commencement-address.

5. Maya Angelou, "Excerpts from the Speech Delivered by Maya Angelou to the Class of 1982 at Wellesley College in Wellesley, Mass." (commencement speech, Wellesley College, Wellesley, Massachusetts, 1982), Wellesley College Website, http://www.wellesley.edu/events/commencement/archives /1982commencement/commencementaddress.

GLOSSARY

Aftercare: Nurturing care and emotional support administered by a dom/me to a sub after any type of physically or mentally challenging BDSM play.

BDSM: An overlapping abbreviation of **B**ondage and **D**iscipline, **D**ominance and **S**ubmission, and **S**adism and **M**asochism. Used interchangeably with "kink" and "S&M," and refers to psychological, spiritual, emotional, physical, sexual, and/or erotic practices.

Body Worship: Physically revering a part of another person's body. Body worship is usually an erotic fetish, and often performed as an act of submission.

Bondage: Any consensual practice involving restraints placed on the body to restrict freedom of movement.

Bondage Horse: A piece of fetish furniture commonly found in BDSM dungeons, designed to position or secure a submissive in preparation for a spanking. Also known as a spanking horse or spanking bench.

Bottom: Someone who takes the passive, receiving, or obedient role in BDSM relationships and/or psychological, sexual, or erotic scene play.

Boundaries: Guidelines, rules, or limits outlined and agreed upon by the parties involved during negotiations of a scene or BDSM relationship.

Bullwhip: A single-tailed whip made of plaited leather.

Checking In: The act of a dominant asking how a submissive feels during a scene, to assist in monitoring the submissive's emotional and physical state.

Collar: A symbol of commitment worn around the neck to indicate one's submissive or slave status in a BDSM relationship or scene.

Contract: A formal or informal documented agreement between a dominant and a submissive that outlines in detail the BDSM relationship.

Crop: Short for riding crop, a short whip used for impact play in BDSM.

Dom/me: Someone who takes the dominant role in a BDSM relationship.

Domination: Consensual control imposed on a submissive by a dominant, through physical and/or verbal means, during a BDSM power exchange.

Dominatrix: A female who takes the dominant role in BDSM relationships and/or psychological, sexual, or erotic scene play. Domme is short for "dominatrix."

Dominant: Someone who takes the dominant or controlling role over the bottom or submissive in BDSM relationships and/or psychological, sexual, or erotic scene play.

Dungeon: BDSM-equipped play spaces or "playrooms" set aside for kink activities. Also called "fetish club" or "playspace."

Dungeon Monitor: Person who oversees the BDSM playspace and play parties, and enforces club rules. Also known as a Dungeon Master.

Fetish: A sexual fixation on a nonsexual object, item of clothing, activity, or body part.

Flogger: A multi-thong whip made of flat strips of leather or other flexible material.

Flogging: Impact play in which a dominant uses a flogger on a submissive.

Hard Limits: A set of boundaries and personal guidelines related to BDSM acts that either the dominant or submissive will absolutely not engage in.

Jane: Author's affectionate, inclusive term for females.

Kink: Consensual erotic practices involving the interplay of power, used interchangeably with BDSM. Author's acronym: **K**ink **I**ntent **N**urtures **K**nowing.

Kink-Think: Kink-inspired wisdom for personal growth.

Kinkster: Someone in the BDSM scene who practices kinky behavior including psychological, spiritual, emotional, physical, sexual, and/or erotic scene play.

Latex (Fetish): The fetishistic attraction to latex wearers or the garments themselves.

Life Spank: Mindful incentive for empowerment.

Lifestyle: Refers to the BDSM community's way of life.

Limits: A set of boundaries and personal guidelines related to BDSM acts that the dominant and/or submissive choose to modify, restrict, or not engage in.

Masochist: Someone who enjoys receiving pain or humiliation, not necessarily sexual or erotic.

Masochism: The eroticism and/or enjoyment of pain.

Master: A man who takes the dominant role in BDSM and controls the activity. Also used as a nongender-specific title for someone with mastery.

Mistress: A female dominant; a term commonly used to address a dominatrix.

No-Limits Submissive: A submissive who chooses not to set limits related to BDSM play rather than negotiate boundaries and personal guidelines.

Nonsexual Play: Style of BDSM play that is intended for personal growth versus erotic arousal. Not interpereted as sexual in nature.

Paddle: A board or other flat-surfaced implement, usually made of leather or wood, used for striking (usually bare) buttocks.

Play: Consensual BDSM activities of a psychological, sexual, emotional, spiritual, physical, or erotic nature. Play occurs during scenes or sessions and/or BDSM relationships.

Play Party: Social events in which kinky (and kink-curious) attendees observe or engage in BDSM scenes and activities.

Pony Play: A combination of BDSM and erotic role-play, usually involving bondage and discipline, that involves the submissive taking on the persona of a pony.

Power Exchange: BDSM activities in which participants take on different levels of consensual power and grant or receive mental or physical control.

Power Play: Used synonymously with power exchange, any BDSM activities in which participants take on different levels of consensual power. Vanilla power play appropriates milder versions of BDSM power play.

Power Poses: Body postures that convey competence and power.

Pup Play: Human-animal role-play in which one person takes on the role of a puppy and another takes on that of the handler or trainer.

Puppy: Someone who enjoys acting as a puppy and submitting to a master during human-animal role-play.

Red: A common safeword used in BDSM to cease activity.

Role-Play: Taking on complementary roles during BDSM play to assist in acting out fantasies.

Sadist: Someone who enjoys inflicting pain or humiliation, not necessarily sexual or erotic.

Sadomasochist: Someone who enjoys activities that involve sadism and masochism.

Safe, Sane, and Consensual: Acceptable play within the BDSM community, using strong principles to guide relationships and activities.

Safeword: An agreed-upon word or phrase used by a submissive to stop a BDSM act or reduce the intensity.

Scene: An encounter or "session" in which BDSM activity takes place. Also used to refer to the BDSM community as a whole.

S&M: Sadism and Masochism (sadomasochism); used interchangeably with BDSM to denote psychological, spiritual, emotional, sexual, and/or erotic power exchange.

Slave: A submissive who consensually surrenders control and grants power to a dominant, master, or owner; sometimes loosely used to refer to a submissive.

Spanking: The act of striking a submissive's (usually bare) buttocks with a bare hand, paddle, or other implement in BDSM play.

Spanking Bench: A piece of fetish furniture commonly found in BDSM dungeons, designed to position or secure a submissive in preparation for a spanking. Also known as a spanking horse or bondage horse.

Soft Limits: A set of boundaries and personal guidelines related to BDSM acts that either the dominant or submissive are ambivalent about engaging in.

Submission: The act of granting power by consent, and taking the obedient, receiving, or bottom role in BDSM relationships and/or scene play.

Submissive: Someone who grants a dominant power by consent, and chooses to take the obedient, receiving, or bottom role in BDSM relationships and/or scene play.

Sub: An abbreviation for submissive.

Subspace: A trance-like state a submissive may experience during BDSM play.

Switch: Someone who switches between the roles of dominance and submission.

Top: Someone who takes the dominant or controlling role over that of the bottom or submissive in BDSM relationships and/or scene play.

Topspace: A trance-like state a dominant (aka "top") may experience during BDSM play.

Training: The act of a dominant modifying a submissive's behavior and/or attitude through instruction. Also refers to the teaching of the BDSM lifestyle, specific BDSM activities, or fundamentals of submission and servitude.

Trampling: A fetish practice in which a prone submissive is walked on and trampled underfoot by a dominant (usually a barefoot female).

Vanilla: Someone who does not self-define as kinky or participate in the BDSM lifestyle. The term "vanilla" refers to a preference for an activity or thing in its traditional state and is based on the traditionally popular vanilla ice cream flavor.

Whip: A long thong-tailed device, made of plaited leather, used for impact play. Common BDSM whips are the stockwhip, bullwhip, single and multi-tail, snakewhip, and quirt.

X-Cross: A stationary bondage frame in the shape of an X, commonly found in BDSM dungeons, designed to position and restrain a submissive in a spread-eagle position. Also known as a St. Andrew's Cross or saltire.

24/7 Power Exchange: A total power exchange in which a submissive consensually surrenders total control indefinitely.

*B*ONUS SCENE: MY FIRST SPANKING

In a sparse playroom too small to swing a cat in, with black-and-white checkerboard tiles, a gold spanking bench, and an X-cross, I got my first lesson in spanking. A domme named Mistress Savannah had taken me under her wing and arranged for me to play with her collared submissive, a sandy blond named Will who followed behind her.

Will was ordered to strip and face the X-cross. His ass was beautiful. Round and firm, the color of milk. It was hard to look away. The mistress cupped it and gave it a few hard smacks with her palm. Then she raised her flogging arm regally, held the tails with the opposing hand, and released the tails with a pop.

Will stood stoic and I squealed. The mistress held out the flogger and reminded me to be careful with the landing position of the falls. "Repeatedly strike the buttocks or other fatty areas to create a build-up of endorphins, before moving to another spot."

I eyed the flogger and studied Will's backside. "Cliff's Notes, please?"

She winked. "Just aim for his ass."

She expertly landed the flogger tails in figure eight's on Will, then handed the whip to me. I took it and cut through the air, making practice loops to get the hang of it, while nervously stalling for time. I'd never struck someone, much less with a flogger.

"William, tell her you want it."

"Please!" he begged. "I want you to."

Will calmly waited. Finally I stepped up, trained the flogger on him and released the swing, snapping the flogger back just as the tails hit him. The act was oddly fulfilling and calmed my worries. Mistress Savannah said, "Pain has its own opulence, don't doubt it," and Will pushed his ass at me, skin faintly reddened.

I thudded the flogger against him again. My aim turned truer and my strikes more sure. Mistress Savannah stood near me, arms crossed and grinning, occasionally giving me pointers and talking about the feeling of connection that is produced in session, and the need that BDSM fulfills.

Then a switch was tripped inside me—as the tails popped and snapped deliciously, each blow ignited me. It was exhilarating; I wanted to own that ass. Will stood tall and steady, arms and legs spread, almost noble in stature.

I sent the tails steadily against him. "Give me that ass," I said, and he arched his back hard. Mistress Savannah laughed.

The rhythm of the flogger slicing through air, the snap of suede against skin, and the intensity were all mesmeric. After a few more figure eight's I slowed the flogger to a stop. "That was amazing! Are you okay, Will?"

Mistress Savannah said, "Don't be too nice to him!" She walked over and smacked him with an open palm. "William, thank her properly."

Will dropped to his knees and elbows, succulent ass raised, and slid his tongue along the length of my boots.

$\mathcal{A}$BOUT THE AUTHOR

Lux Alani took a dominatrix detour that transformed her vanilla life. She practices radical openness to empowerment, and her journey from vanilla to dominatrix and back is spank-full of insights. Lux has been a crisis counselor, international model, cultural activist, and derby girl. Her mission is to inspire sacred feminine badasses!